T0305288

Post Keynesian Theory and Policy

NEW DIRECTIONS IN POST-KEYNESIAN ECONOMICS

Series Editors: Louis-Philippe Rochon, *Laurentian University, Sudbury, Canada* and Sergio Rossi, *University of Fribourg, Switzerland*

Post-Keynesian economics is a school of thought inspired by the work of John Maynard Keynes, but also by Michal Kalecki, Joan Robinson, Nicholas Kaldor and other Cambridge economists, for whom money and effective demand are essential to explain economic activity. The aim of this series is to present original research work (single or co-authored volumes as well as edited books) that advances Post-Keynesian economics at both theoretical and policy-oriented levels.

Areas of research include, but are not limited to, monetary and financial economics, macro and microeconomics, international economics, development economics, economic policy, political economy, analyses of income distribution and financial crises, and the history of economic thought.

Post Keynesian Theory and Policy

A Realistic Analysis of the Market Oriented Capitalist Economy

Paul Davidson

Holly Chair of Excellence Emeritus, University of Tennessee, USA and Founding Editor of the Journal of Post Keynesian Economics

NEW DIRECTIONS IN POST-KEYNESIAN ECONOMICS

Edward Elgar
PUBLISHING

Cheltenham, UK • Northampton, MA, USA

© Paul Davidson 2015

All rights reserved. No part of this publication may be reproduced, stored in a retrieval system or transmitted in any form or by any means, electronic, mechanical or photocopying, recording, or otherwise without the prior permission of the publisher.

Published by
Edward Elgar Publishing Limited
The Lypiatts
15 Lansdown Road
Cheltenham
Glos GL50 2JA
UK

Edward Elgar Publishing, Inc.
William Pratt House
9 Dewey Court
Northampton
Massachusetts 01060
USA

A catalogue record for this book
is available from the British Library

Library of Congress Control Number: 2015935899

This book is available electronically in the **Elgar**online
Economics subject collection
DOI 10.4337/9781784718251

ISBN 978 1 78471 824 4 (cased)
ISBN 978 1 78471 825 1 (eBook)

Typeset by Columns Design XML Ltd, Reading
Printed and bound in Great Britain by T.J. International Ltd, Padstow

Contents

1. Did anyone notice the global financial crisis of 2007–2008?   1
2. Alternative theories of the operation of a capitalist economy   6
3. Unemployment and the classical theory's axioms   14
4. Keynes–Post Keynesian theory: money and money
   contracts   28
5. Why traditional mainstream Keynesian theory is not
   Keynes's theory   41
6. Creating full employment policies   53
7. Inflation policy   63
8. Securitization, liquidity and market failure   77
9. Globalization, international trade and international
   payments   92
10. Is international free trade always beneficial?   124
11. Policies to assure a civilized capitalist economic system   136

Index   145

1. Did anyone notice the global financial crisis of 2007–2008?

On November 4, 2008, at the dedication of a new building, Queen Elizabeth of Great Britain visited the London School of Economics (LSE). While there she was given a briefing by academics at the LSE on the origins and effects of the global financial crisis and its resulting turmoil in international financial markets. The Queen is reported to have asked, "Why did nobody notice it developing?" The director of research at LSE told her, "At every stage someone was relying on somebody else and everyone thought they were doing the right thing."

How is it possible that the many intelligent investors, bankers, brokers, fund managers and other financial market participants thought they were doing the right thing, when it is clear in hindsight that market activity was creating a situation that ultimately caused global financial markets to collapse?

The answer lies in the fact that, for at least four decades, the economic theory that has dominated academic teaching has not been applicable to our economic system. This theory's teachings affected the economic reasoning of economic students who then became bankers, entrepreneurs, politicians, government regulators and so on. This theory is a fairy tale fable that has no descriptive relationship with the operations of our market oriented, money using, capitalist economy. Consequently, what was seen as a way of doing good in this fairy tale economy, created destructive economic forces in the world in which we live.

There were a few economists, however, that had a better understanding of how the modern market economy works. They did notice that financial markets were creating an unstable situation that, sooner or later, was going to cause a terrible financial markets problem. These economists called themselves Post Keynesians since they used and further developed the general theory that the

English economist John Maynard Keynes had originated in 1936 to explain why the financial crisis precipitated by the New York Stock Market collapse in 1929 had created "the great depression" that encompassed the global economic system for years.

As early as 2002, in my Post Keynesian book *Financial Markets, Money and the Real World*,[1] I noted that in modern market economies, the development of new well-organized markets for financial assets severed any direct link between the investment demand decision by entrepreneurs for the purchase of fixed capital plant and equipment and the savers' desire to earn as much as possible on their savings by making portfolio composition decisions (involving the ownership of financial assets including equities, debts, etc.).

The existence of well-organized financial markets, however, is a potential double-edged sword. The good edge of the sword is that such markets typically facilitate the transfer of funds which permits command over existing real resources from savers who do not want to use their funds today to buy things; to others, including investors, who want to obtain things in excess of what their own income earning claims would permit. In exchange, savers receive liquid financial assets such as stocks, bonds, mutual funds and so on in which they store their savings and hopefully earn more income while holding these assets in their portfolio of savings. These financial assets are deemed to be liquid in the sense that the savers believe that these financial assets can be readily sold for cash when, any time in the future, they wish to make a fast exit and return their savings to a cash reserve.

This good edge facilitates financing more capital goods investment including very large investment projects – projects often too large to be funded by any single individual or small group of partners. In so doing, the resulting investment projects typically increase productivity and reduce the costs of producing new goods and services for households to purchase.

The bad edge of the sword is that, in circumstances when many holders of these financial assets suddenly have increasing fears about what may happen in the uncertain future, the liquidity of these financial assets can evaporate as potential buyers disappear from the market. The result can be severe economic liquidity and insolvency problems that can engulf the global financial community.

When regulators of the financial market permitted financial institutions to bundle together many illiquid mortgage debts to create mortgage backed derivatives (which encompassed subprime mortgages[2] in the mix) to then sell at a profit to savers, the seeds of financial catastrophe were being sowed.[3] Savers were told that these securitized derivatives would provide holders with a larger return than could be obtained elsewhere (another apparent good) while these securities would maintain liquidity and be easily sold for cash.

This securitization process allowed many subprime mortgages to be bundled together with more conventional mortgages. This securitized bundling appeared to reduce the risk of an overall bad financial investment by savers since there would still be many in-good-standing mortgages in the bundle. Accordingly, these derivative securities were considered to be doing a social good in that more subprime mortgage loans could be made to allow many people to buy the homes they otherwise could not afford. Simultaneously, these derivative assets promised saver-holders of these derivative financial assets a larger rate of return than they could obtain by putting their savings elsewhere (e.g., into a money market account or even buying US government bonds) – another apparent good.

Since the initial packager of these securitized derivatives typically advertised that these financial assets were "as good as cash," that is, were readily liquidated for money in the market, the purchasers of these derivatives did not fear any significant loss if, and when, they decided to make a fast exit and sell their holdings of these derivatives. Moreover, rating agencies that profess to provide an objective report to the general public of the creditworthiness of such securitized financial assets gave these mortgage backed derivatives an AAA rating that further encouraged savers to believe that these derivatives were a safe investment for their funds.

No wonder, as the LSE director told the Queen, "everyone thought they were doing the right thing" for themselves and their economic community. But in 2007 these derivative and other new securitized markets appeared to collapse as many holders of these derivative securities became bearish and suddenly wanted to sell to make a fast exit from the market while no one apparently wanted to buy these derivatives offered for sale. The result was a liquidity crisis as these derivatives, now recognized as "toxic assets," lost all market value in the absence of sufficient buyers (bulls).

Accounting rules require that securities that are liquid and are held in one's balance sheet must be valued at the current market price on the asset side of the balance sheet. Since these toxic assets were held not only by individuals but also across the global financial community by bankers, pension funds and other institutional funds, the asset side of the balance sheets of these institutions collapsed, thereby damaging or destroying the accounting value of the net worth of the holders of these assets. The resulting financial crisis did not spare any important national economy.

In my book *Financial Markets, Money and the Real World* I noted that a financial crisis was likely to occur in the near future. I wrote that in the United States:

> Recent trends in the growth of mutual funds and other nonbank financial intermediaries have encouraged saver households to reallocate their saving portfolio from holding (government insured) bank deposits towards holding more liabilities [issued by] nonbank financial intermediaries. This has permitted a significant expansion of debt obligations on the part of debtor households and enterprises. This suggests that a sudden switch by many [portfolio holding savers] ... to a fast exit strategy at a future date could cause a horrific liquidity problem.[4]

The global financial crisis of 2007–2008 indicates how prophetic this 2002 Post Keynesian message proved to be.

As we will discuss in later chapters, the Post Keynesian analytical system can suggest ways to dull the bad edge of liquid financial markets swords via (1) legislating proper regulatory rules on financial markets and (2) having central banks ready to alleviate a financial liquidity crisis if it still occurs. Accordingly, a major purpose of this book is to explain, not only to Queen Elizabeth but to all, why what is the mainstream's fairy tale classical economic theory is still being espoused by the talking head "experts" and "elites" on TV and in governments, central banks and even international institutions such as the International Monetary Fund (IMF), while, though still often ignored, the Post Keynesian approach is available to provide a realistic analysis of the operation of the money using capitalist economy in which we live. Once we understand the operation of a 21st-century market oriented, money using world economy as explained by Post Keynesian analysis, we shall then understand why the policies necessary to deal with economic problems when they occur will be significantly different than those often espoused by such elite experts.

NOTES

1. P. Davidson, *Financial Markets, Money and the Real World* (Edward Elgar, Cheltenham, UK and Northampton, MA, 2002) Chapter 6.
2. A subprime mortgage is a loan made to individuals to help purchase a home. These individuals typically are poor credit risks, often are unable to prove income earnings and possess few, if any, other assets that can be pledged as collateral. The sub prime loan typically involves high origination fees, prepayment penalties, balloon maturities and other costs that make it difficult to refinance the loan if interest rates decline. Often the loan comes with an artificially low introductory rate that ratchets upward substantially thereby increasing monthly payments by as much as 50 percent.

   The good was that these subprime loans increased opportunities for home ownership, adding nine million US households to the number of homeowners in the decade from 1996 to 2006. Often this permitted the poor to gain the American Dream of home ownership.

   The bad is that when monthly payments rose on these types of loans the default rate became very large.
3. At this point we illustrate the problem with the securitization of mortgage backed derivative securities. But at the same time, other exotic securities such as credit default swaps were being invested and sold to the public which had similar faults.
4. Op. cit., p. 117.

2. Alternative theories of the operation of a capitalist economy

The financial crisis that began in 2007–2008 started as a small default problem on some subprime mortgages that had been issued in the United States. These defaulting subprime mortgages were part of the mix in mortgage backed derivatives. As a result, holders of these derivatives began to fear that the mortgages in their specific derivative financial asset holdings might also soon fall into default. Consequently, many derivative asset holders tried to make fast exits from the markets for such assets as the fear of potential defaults spread. With many holders rushing to exit the market while few or none were willing to buy more of these assets, the market prices of derivatives crashed. The result was to reduce the asset side of balance sheets of institutions that held these derivatives to the point of insolvency. This effect quickly ballooned globally into the largest threat to economic prosperity since the Great Depression. What is rarely noted is that the origin of this latest global financial market crisis, like the New York Stock Exchange crash of 1929 that appears to have precipitated the Great Depression, is associated with the operation of free financial markets unhampered by government regulations.

In recent decades, many mainstream academic economists, central bankers, most policy makers in government and their economic advisers have advocated freeing financial markets from government rules and regulators. These free market advocates insist that (1) government regulation of markets and large government spending policies are the cause of our economic problems and (2) ending big government and freeing markets from regulatory controls are the solutions to our economic problems.

In an amazing "mea culpa" testimony before the House Committee on Oversight and Government Reform on October 23, 2008, Alan Greenspan, the former Chair of the Federal Reserve System and a strong advocate of unregulated markets, admitted that he had overestimated the ability of free financial markets to self-correct. He indicated that he had entirely missed the possibility that deregulation could unleash a destructive force on the economy. In his testimony, Greenspan stated:

> This crisis, however, has turned out to be much broader than I could have imagined. ... those of us who had looked to the self interest of lending institutions to protect shareholders' equity (myself especially) are in a state of shocked disbelief. ... In recent decades a vast risk management and pricing system has evolved, combining the best insights of mathematicians and finance experts supported by major advances in computer and communications technology. A Nobel Prize [in economics] was awarded for the discovery of the [free market] pricing model that underpins much of the advance in [financial] derivatives markets. This modern risk management paradigm held sway for decades. The whole intellectual edifice, however, collapsed.

Under questioning by members of the House Committee on Oversight and Government Reform, Greenspan admitted:

> I found a flaw in the models that I perceive is the critical functioning structure that defines how the world works. That's precisely the reason I was shocked ... I still do not fully understand why it happened, and obviously to the extent that I figure it happened and why, I shall change my views.

We shall explain to Greenspan and other elites the flaw in their theory, explaining how the "functioning structure" of the world market economic and financial system works.

THEORY PROVIDES EXPLANATION

Since biblical times, humans have tried to understand the things they observe happening around them. In general, the human mind believes that there must be a cause for any event we observe. For most of the history of mankind, human belief attributed to the design of God, or the Gods, the cause of anything that happened.

Beginning in the 17th century, philosophers began to argue that explanations of observed events could be developed on the basis of reasoning of the mind. In this intellectual movement that historians called the Age of Reason or Enlightenment, order and regularity was seen to come from human analysis of observed phenomena. The power of truth was not in the possession of truth but in its acquisition. The goal was to understand and explain observed processes occurring in our world. To this end, it was essential to develop theories that would explain observed phenomena.

Any understanding of the world we observe will be the creation of the human mind. Reasoning involves the mind creating a theory to explain what people observe happening. A theory is essentially the way humans attempt to explain observed phenomena on the basis of a logical model that is built on the foundation of some fundamental axioms. An axiom is an assumption that the theorist model builder accepts as a self-evident universal truth that does not have to be proven. From this axiomatic foundation, the theorist uses the laws of logic to reach one or more conclusions. In economics these conclusions are presented to the public as the explanation of economic events that are occurring, or will occur, in our world of experience. The theory can then be used to suggest what can, or cannot, be done to affect economic outcomes. If the facts of experience conflict with what are the logical conclusions of one's economic theory, as Greenspan admits happened in his theory of financial markets, then one or more of the theory's fundamental axioms are flawed. The theory is unrealistic and should be discarded so a different, more realistic theory can be built. The alternative to developing a better theory would be to change the facts – or even one's definition of the facts – to fit the unrealistic theory.[1]

No theory is ever accepted as the final explanation. Rather, theories are accepted until they are supplanted by "better" theories. Typically, the better theory requires fewer restrictive axioms for its foundation than the older theory it replaces.

One can consider the builder of an economic theory as if he/she is a magician. Theorists rarely make logical errors in moving from axioms to conclusions any more than a professional prestidigitator drops the deck of cards while performing a card trick. Most economics theorists are proficient at creating the illusion of pulling policy conclusion rabbits out of their black hat model. Often the policy rabbits pulled from the black hat generate some audience enjoyment and applause.

A careful examination of the (axiomatic) rabbits the magician put initially into the black hat back stage is required to evaluate the relevance of the policy rabbits pulled from the black hat on stage. Before accepting the logical conclusions of any economic theory as correct and therefore applicable to our market oriented, money using, economic system, central bankers such as Alan Greenspan as well as government officials, business executives, politicians and the general public should examine and be prepared to question the fundamental axioms of any theory. If these axioms are not applicable to our economic world, then the policy conclusions must be rejected as irrelevant and even possibly harmful.

ALTERNATIVE THEORIES

There are two fundamental economic theories that attempt to explain the operation of a market oriented, money using, capitalist economy. These are:

1. The classical economic theory that has tended to reign supreme in economic circles since the latter part of the 18th century. There are many versions of this classical theory. These go under different names but are all based on the same axiomatic foundation. The labels for these versions include efficient market theory, Walrasian theory, general equilibrium theory, dynamic general equilibrium theory, Austrian theory *and* mainstream "Keynesian" theories, including the neo-classical synthesis Keynesian theory developed by Nobel Prize winner Paul Samuelson and the New Keynesian theory developed by students of the Samuelson neoclassical synthesis Keynesian approach. The proponents of these variants of the classical axiomatic analysis may differ on the details of their analysis, but the mantra of all these approaches is that, in the long run, if markets possess freely flexible wages and product prices, then these markets will ultimately assure a fully employed economy that provides as much prosperity as its resources can produce.
2. The Keynes–Post Keynesian liquidity theory of a market oriented economy where business entrepreneurs make all important production decisions. The conclusion of this theory

is that the government can cure, with the cooperation of private industry and households, some major economic flaws that can occur in the operation of a capitalist market oriented economy when, in the absence of government action, unfettered greed and/or fear is permitted to dominate economic decisions.

CLASSICAL ECONOMIC THEORY AND SAY'S LAW

Underlying the various classical theories is the implicit belief in the applicability to all market economies of something economists call Say's Law. The 19th-century economic proposition known as Say's Law is the foundation of the classical argument that a competitive market with flexible wages and prices is the mechanism that assures that market forces will inevitably bring the economy to a situation where all resources will be fully employed. All who want to work can and will find a job with profit oriented business firms and without any government help or interference. The result will be an economy that provides the highest level of prosperity the system can support given its natural resources, its workforce population and its level of innovative entrepreneurs.

Say's Law evolved from the writings of a French economist, Jean Baptiste Say, who in 1803 stated that "products always exchange for products." In 1808, the English economist James Mill translated Say's French language dictum as "supply creates its own demand." Mill's phraseology has since been established in economics as Say's Law.

A simple argument suggesting why Say's Law appeals to classical economic theorists is as follows: The sole explanation of why people are willing to work to produce goods and services is to earn income by supplying these goods and services for sale in the market. For all persons engaged in income earning productive activities, the activity is presumed to be disagreeable or unpleasant compared to using the same time to pursue pleasurable leisure activities. People, however, do obtain pleasure (utility) from the purchase and consumption of producible goods and services. People, therefore, will be willing to engage in the activity of working and producing goods and services only if they can earn sufficient income for each unit of work effort to buy enough products of industry to provide themselves sufficient pleasure to more than offset the unpleasantness of their income earning production efforts.

Income earning producers would not be maximizing their individual economic welfare if they engaged in the disagreeable act of contributing to the production process in order to earn income while these income earners did not intend to spend every penny that they currently earn on pleasure yielding goods and services produced by industry.

Say's Law presumes that if people have their own self-interest in mind and wish to maximize the utility or happiness they obtain from their economic endeavors, then all income earned in the market from the production and sales of goods and services will be spent immediately to buy (demand) pleasurable goods and services produced by industry. The supply (production) of new goods and services always produces sufficient income and demand to buy all things that are produced. There is never a lack of effective market demand for all the products that an economy can produce when it fully employs its workers who want to spend all they earn on produced goods and services.

In other words, business firms hire all the workers who want to work to produce goods and services for profitable sale in the market. All the income earned by workers, managers and business owners is then spent in the market to buy the produced goods and services. There will never be anything produced that cannot be profitably sold to income earners, that is, there can never be a lack of demand for the product of industry and its workers. Full employment and the highest possible prosperity will develop according to this doctrine called Say's Law.

Writing in 1936, in the midst of the Great Depression where there was massive unemployment and businesses could not find buyers for many of the products they produced, Keynes declared that Say's Law

> is not the true law relating the aggregate demand [for goods and services with the aggregate] ... supply function [of goods and services produced]. If, however, this is not the true law, there is a vitally important chapter of economic theory that remains to be written and without which all discussions concerning the volume of aggregate employment are futile.[2]

With this declaration that the Say's Law homily saying everything supplied in an economy created its own demand was not a "true law," Keynes set himself the task to explain why Say's Law is not applicable to the economic world of experience. Keynes produced a theory that would explain why there could be massive unemployment even in a competitive market economy with flexible wages and prices. In essence, Keynes claimed that he could provide a general theory of employment to explain why an increase in supply (produced by workers in industry) did not create automatically an equivalent increase in demand for the products of industry. The problem was that some of the fundamental axioms underlying the classical theory advocated by most of the "experts" professing classical economic theory were not applicable to the world in which we lived. As Keynes stated:

> The classical theorists resemble Euclidean geometers in a non-Euclidean world who, discovering that in experience straight lines apparently parallel often meet, rebuke the lines for not keeping straight – as the only remedy for the unfortunate collisions which are occurring. Yet, in truth, there is no remedy except to overthrow the axiom of parallels and to work out a non-Euclidean geometry. Something similar is required today in economics.[3]

By overthrowing three restrictive classical axioms, Keynes developed a general theory that was equivalent to his call for a non-Euclidean economics. (The three classical axioms will be discussed in the following chapters.) Keynes argued that these classical axioms were not applicable to the monetary economy in which we live, where entrepreneurs organize the production process by hiring workers to produce goods and services to be profitably sold for money in the market place. The collision of apparently straight parallel lines in a non-Euclidean world was the equivalent of classical economists observing massive unemployment in their world while their theory suggested that the market should provide full employment for all who want to work. To the extent that these classical theory economists had to explain unemployment, they argued that the unemployed workers were at fault for not being willing to accept a job at a lower market wage where all could be fully employed. In other words, the victims (unemployed workers) were blamed for their unemployment!

Keynes suggested that it was not the refusal of workers to accept a lower wage for getting employment that was the problem. Classical economic theory which professes that if workers would only accept lower wages all who wanted to work would be employed was not applicable to our economic system. Keynes argued that classical theory was a theory whose "teaching is misleading and disastrous if we attempt to apply it to the facts of experience."[4]

Unfortunately, even in our time many so-called experts in economics – including Nobel Prize winners – continue to develop sophisticated models that still possess the fundamental axioms of classical economic theory that Keynes argued had to be discarded. Since these classical axioms lie below a mountain of mathematical and statistical computer analysis, they are difficult for the average person, or even many classically trained economists, to recognize. Nevertheless, the results of using these very technical classical axiomatic models have created decisions by policy makers and regulators that are often misleading and disastrous – as Alan Greenspan admitted in his Congressional testimony.

NOTES

1. I must admit that sometimes such changes to the facts happen in academia. For example, see Chapter 4 for a discussion of Milton Friedman's change to the definition of savings in his permanent income theory to get the redefined facts to support his classical analysis and Say's Law.
2. J. M. Keynes, *The General Theory of Employment, Interest and Money* (Macmillan, London, 1936) p. 26.
3. Op. cit., p. 16.
4. Op. cit., p. 3.

3. Unemployment and the classical theory's axioms

John Maynard Keynes wrote, "the ideas of economists and political philosophers, both when they are right and when they are wrong, are more powerful than is commonly understood. Indeed the world is ruled by little else."[1] The ideas embodied in classical economic theory continue to rule the economic policy decisions of government officials and central bankers despite Alan Greenspan's admission that he does not know why his classical economic theory failed to recognize the possibility of the global financial crisis of 2007–2008 and since then the failure of developed economies to rapidly recover from what is now often called the "Great Recession." In this chapter we will examine the axiomatic foundation of classical economic theory's ideas and their subsequent application to the economic world in which we live. More often these classical ideas have encouraged the adoption of policies that have led to economic events that have failed to resolve our economic problems and have, at times, resulted in worsening the economic distress.

The classical theory rests on the premise that all free markets in a capitalist system are perfect and all-wise. Accordingly, the market can and will solve any economic problems that may arise due to some shock to the system. For example, classical theory argues that when wages are perfectly flexible, if unemployment should occur, then the market wage would almost instantaneously decline. This wage decline would offer entrepreneurs in every industry more profit opportunities as the labor costs of product would be lower. The lower labor cost would permit firms to sell more products at a lower price and still make profits. Consequently, classical theory insists that at some lower market money wage all who wanted to work at that wage would be employed and all they produced would be profitably sold.

In the classical system, unemployment could persist only if workers refused to accept the lower money wage that assured full employment. Unions tend to prevent workers from accepting wage reductions. Minimum wage legislation also can prevent reducing market wages. The result will be that any rigidity or stickiness in money wages that prevents wages from falling will prevent the market from providing full employment with profitable sales of products. In this classical analysis, the villains that prevent the markets from assuring a persistent full employment economy are unions, minimum wage laws and workers truculence to accept lower money wages.

Winston Churchill once said, "No one pretends that democracy is perfect or all-wise. Indeed, it has been said that democracy is the worst form of government except for all those other forms that have been tried from time to time." Keynes's theory of the operation of our market oriented, money using economy suggests a message regarding market capitalism that is similar to Churchill's message about democracy. Keynes would suggest that no one should pretend that market oriented capitalism is perfect or all-wise, though, despite its faults, it is typically better than any other form of economic system that has been tried.

Keynes wrote that, "The outstanding faults of the economic society in which we live are its failure to provide full employment and its arbitrary and inequitable distribution of income and wealth."[2] Keynes's theory, however, can explain that it is not the stickiness of wages that causes unemployment and income and wealth inequalities in the normal operations of a market oriented entrepreneurial system. Once the true causes of such faults are known, then the theory can suggest policies that can solve, or at least reduce the severity of, these major flaws of a capitalist economy.

THE CLASSICAL AXIOMS THAT KEYNES OVERTHREW

Let us examine the classical theory axioms that Keynes claimed prevented classical theory from providing a useful explanation of the operation of our market oriented economic system. The three classical axioms that had to be overthrown to provide a more relevant explanation of the operation of our economy are (1) the ergodic axiom, (2) the neutral money axiom and (3) the gross substitution axiom.

The Ergodic Axiom

Time is a device that prevents all things from happening at once. Any economic decision made at any moment in time will have its outcome (payout) minutes, hours, days, weeks, months or even years in the future. Given all possible alternative actions that one can choose in the market place at any moment in time, how can a self-interested decision maker choose the specific alternative action that will provide him/her with the best income or pleasure in the forthcoming future? Only if the decision maker knows precisely what the future outcome of any possible decision will be can the choice of the optimum decision always be made.

By various different methods, classical theory presumes self-interested decision makers already "know" precisely what the pay-off in the future will be as a result of any specific decision taken today. Consequently, classical theory assumes all actions taken by people in the market place are in the best interests of each self-interested decision maker to promote his/her economic position in the future that all know will be forthcoming. The result is that all the economy's resources are efficiently allocated towards the processes of production and exchange which yield the highest possible returns in the known future of markets for every inhabitant of the economy. In other words, all markets are assumed efficient. It is this presumed efficiency of all financial markets that led Alan Greenspan to believe before 2007 that the global financial crisis of 2007–2008 could not have happened.

In 19th-century classical economic theory, it was usually merely assumed that all individuals "knew" the future with perfect certainty. In the late 19th century, French economist Léon Walras set out a mathematical deterministic system of equations as the most extensive description of the old classical theory of perfect certainty. In this Walrasian system, markets exist for people to enter into contracts for transactions to buy and/or sell today (i.e., spot markets) and transactions to buy and sell for every possible future date (i.e., forward markets). Walras assumed there was a market auctioneer for all these spot and forward markets who provided every participant today with complete information about every market outcome from here to eternity. Thus, each market participant in the Walrasian system always knew the future.

In the 20th century, economists Kenneth Arrow and Gerard Debreu formulated the Walrasian system where, in addition to spot and forward markets for all goods and services, they incorporated a complete set of contingency markets. Accordingly, all market transactions could be insured against all possible accidental damaging contingencies.

Ultimately, this type of classical analysis to explain why all market participants know the future led to the theory of "rational expectations" developed by Nobel Prize Laureate Robert Lucas of the University of Chicago. Lucas attempted to use modern probability theory (technically known as stochastic theory) to explain how people in the market through their expectations "know" the future.

In this rational expectations analysis all future outcomes are presumed to be governed by an objective probability distribution.[3] The only question becomes how do decision makers today form their expectations about the objective probability distributions that govern all future outcomes? Lucas postulated that if self-interested individuals are rational humans, then their expectations must be "rational" in the sense that these expectations provide correct information about the probabilities that will govern all outcomes in the future. In Lucas's terminology, the subjective probability distribution about any future date's outcomes that exists in a rational person's mind today is assumed to be equal to the objective probability distribution that actually will govern that future date's outcomes.

How can people obtain information today to form these rational (assumed correct) expectations about all future probabilities associated with any given future date? Statisticians tell us that if characteristics (descriptions) about any event or outcome are governed by a stochastic (probability) process, then knowledge about these characteristics can be obtained. All that is required to make statistically reliable forecasts about the characteristics of any specific dated outcomes is for the analyst to draw a sample from the type of events at those future dates and statistically analyze the sample data obtained.

Since drawing a sample from events occurring in the future is impossible, the assumption that the economy is governed by an *ergodic stochastic process* (i.e., the ergodic axiom) permits the analyst to assert that samples drawn from past or current market data are equivalent to drawing samples from the future market data. In other words, the ergodic axiom in essence presumes the probability distribution that governed past and current economic outcomes will be the same as the probability distribution that governs all future outcomes. Thus, given the ergodic axiom, information about the predetermined future exists today and can be obtained simply by analyzing the statistical outcomes of past probabilistic events. This does not preclude an economy that is moving or changing over time. It does mean all future movements and changes are already predetermined by the characteristics (parameters) of the past and current system.

One of the leaders of this rational expectations school of economic theory, and a Nobel Prize winner, Thomas Sargent, has suggested that this rational expectations economic theory model may be very different from the world of experience. Sargent has written that the rational expectations theory

> imputes to the people inside the model much *more knowledge about* the system they are operating in than is available to the economist or econometrician who is using the model to try to understand their behavior. In particular, an econometrician faces the problem of *estimating* probability distributions and laws of motion that the agents in the model are assumed to know.[4]

If, however, one accepts the ergodic axiom[5] as the foundation of classical economic theory, then it is easy to illustrate why government policies cannot improve the future outcomes from what will happen if no government action is taken. Indeed, under this ergodic axiom, all government policy interference in the market can do is to make things worse.

As an illustration, let us examine the science of astronomy, which utilizes the ergodic axiom as a foundation of its theory. The theory of astronomy accepted by all astronomers is that since the moment of the "Big Bang" creation of the universe, the future paths of all the heavenly bodies are predetermined by natural immutable laws that cannot be changed by any human action. By using past data measurements of velocity and direction of heavenly bodies, astronomers can predict accurately, within a few seconds, when and where the next solar eclipse will be visible on earth. Congress, or a Parliament, cannot pass an enforceable law to eliminate the next solar eclipse in order to increase the amount of sunshine the earth receives so as to increase total agricultural production and thereby improve the gross domestic product (GDP) of the economy.

Similarly, if the ergodic axiom applies to our economy, then just as the government cannot legislate changes in solar eclipses, government policies will not be able to legislate changes in economic outcomes already determined by the objective probability distributions governing past and future events. Accepting the ergodic axiom implies the philosophy of *laissez-faire*, that is, government should never interfere in markets since it cannot change the long-run path of the economy any more than legislation can prevent future solar eclipses from occurring.

If one accepts the claim that the economic system is governed by an ergodic stochastic process, then reliable information about the future can be obtained by analyzing samples from the past. This information will permit people to make the correct decisions in the market to maximize the welfare of everyone in the community. Consequently, classical theory declares that the market is efficient in the use of the resources of the economy.

Lawrence Summers, former Secretary of the Treasury and economic adviser to President Obama, has stated that "the ultimate social functions [of efficient markets] are spreading risks, guiding the investment of scarce capital, and processing and disseminating the information [about the future] possessed by diverse traders. ... prices will always reflect fundamental values ... . The logic of efficient markets is compelling."[6]

The logic of the efficient market theory is compelling *if* one accepts the ergodic axiom. For financial markets to be efficient under the Summers' vision, participants must know future revenues and profits that will be associated with the enterprises underlying the securities. These known future revenues associated with the firm's use of productive capital are captured in what Summers calls today's "fundamentals." If financial markets are so efficient, then how does one explain that the financial markets for mortgage backed derivatives, after operating supposedly efficiently for several years, suddenly collapsed in 2007 and thereby brought about the financial market crisis of 2007–2008? As Alan Greenspan found out, it is difficult to explain if, under the ergodic axiom, market are efficient. In later chapters it will be more readily explained when we lay out Keynes's theory of liquidity in a nonergodic economic system.

Keynes did not believe in a predetermined ergodic economic future that cannot be changed for the better by the proper human economic policy actions. Keynes criticized classical theory where

> fact and expectations were assumed to be given in a definite form and risks ... were supposed to be capable of an exact actuarial computation. The calculus of probability ... was supposed capable of reducing uncertainty to the same calculable state as that of certainty itself. ... I accuse the classical economic theory of being itself one of those pretty, polite techniques which tries to deal with the present by abstracting from the fact we know very little about the future. ... [Every classical economist] has overlooked the precise nature of the difference his abstraction makes between theory and practice and the character of the fallacies into which he is likely to be led.[7]

Keynes argued that

> the fact [is] that our knowledge of the future is fluctuating, vague, and uncertain ... By "uncertain" I do not mean merely to distinguish what is known for certain from what is only probable. The game of roulette is not subject, in this sense, to uncertainty. ... About these [future economic outcomes] matters there is no scientific basis on which to form any calculable probability.[8]

The statistical theory of ergodic stochastic processes was developed by the Moscow School of Probability in 1935 and did not become widely known and popular in Western Europe or the United States until after the Second World War and Keynes had died. Consequently, Keynes never knew of or used the ergodic taxonomy in his emphasis on the importance of uncertainty and liquidity in the economic system. Nevertheless, it is clear from his writings that he believed the historical economic data generated in the market place had characteristics that made it nonergodic.[9] Accordingly, probabilities calculated from samples drawn from the past should not be viewed as actuarial information about future events. Or, as Nobel Prize winner Sir John Hicks wrote, "One must assume that people in one's model [theory] do not know what is going to happen, and know that they do not know what is going to happen. As in history."[10]

Keynes believed that intelligent action by government could reduce, if not completely eliminate, the major flaws of the capitalist economy in which we live. Accordingly, Keynes had to overthrow the ergodic axiom and build a theory that was applicable to a world where the economic system was not ergodic and *laissez-faire* was not an applicable philosophy.

Unfortunately, all mainstream economic theorists, whether they label themselves Classical Theorists, Monetarists, Old Neoclassical Synthesis Keynesians or even New Keynesians, still require their theories to be based on the ergodic axiom so that immutable objective probability distributions govern past as well as future events.[11] The aforementioned "Keynesians" (e.g., Nobel Laureates Paul Samuelson, Robert Solow, Paul Krugman and Joseph Stiglitz) still have the ergodic axiom as a foundation in their Old and New Keynesian theories while advocating government policy actions rather than inaction. They justify their recommendation of government taking immediate policy actions on the basis that (1) in the short run wages and prices are not sufficiently flexible and therefore it takes too long for a Walrasian type classical system to readjust after a shock that causes unemployment or (2) there is asymmetric information existing today so that some market participants are fools who are not smart enough to know how to obtain the correct information about the future objective probability distributions from data that exists today. These fools keep making wrong decisions in the market. These wrong decisions cause recessions and depressions.

In essence, these self-proclaimed Keynesians really are Classical Theorists who are impatient with the time they believe it takes the market to reestablish a full employment position. They want government action immediately. As we will see in forthcoming chapters, these "Keynesians" apparently never completely understood the general theory that Keynes developed. Accordingly, it was left to the Post Keynesians to revive Keynes's actual theory and develop its contents to be applicable for our modern, market oriented, money using, entrepreneurial economy.

The Neutral Money Axiom

It follows from the ergodic axiom that the future path of total production and employment in any hypothetical ergodic economic system is predetermined and immutable – just as the future path of heavenly bodies is in astronomy. In any future calendar period in an ergodic system, if the total production of goods and services is predetermined then the neutral money axiom necessarily follows. This axiom asserts that any increase in the quantity of money supplied will have no effect on the (predetermined) total output produced (GDP) or employment in that future period.

Milton Friedman, the Nobel Prize Laureate, is closely associated with the quantity theory of money, a theory which imposes the neutral money axiom so that changes in the quantity of money directly affect changes in the price level. Friedman has described his belief in the neutral money axiom as follows:

> We have accepted the quantity theory presumption ... that changes in the quantity of money as such *in the long run* have a negligible effect on real income, so that nonmonetary forces are "all that matter" for changes in real income [total production or GDP] over the decades and "money does not matter". On the other hand, we have regarded the quantity of money ... as all that matter for ... the price level.[12]

Oliver Blanchard, who is the economics adviser to the IMF and was also a professor at the Massachusetts Institute of Technology's economics department and a researcher at the prestigious National Bureau of Economic Research, has characterized all the mainstream models widely used by economists at government agencies, central banks, in academia, etc. as follows: "All the models we have seen impose the neutrality of money as a maintained assumption. This is very much a matter of faith, based on theoretical considerations rather than on empirical evidence."[13]

Given the volume of real output of goods and services produced in any future period in an ergodic system, if the government (or the central bank) increases the money supply that can be spent on produced goods and services the only effect will be that of inflation, that is, the price of the predetermined level of produced goods and services will rise. Or, as Milton Friedman was fond of saying, "Inflation occurs when too much money is chasing too few goods." For example, if total production (GDP) is scheduled ergodically to rise by 3 percent per annum then, Friedman would argue, the money supply should increase by only 3 percent annually. Accordingly, Friedman's belief that real output has a long-term tendency to grow at 3 percent per annum results in a Friedman policy of a 3 percent rule for money supply growth rather than leaving it to the discretion of central bankers as to how much of a change in the money supply should occur in any period. Money supply changes by more than 3 percent in this example must result in inflation.

Thus, when the Federal Reserve began its policy of creating money by buying huge quantities of government bonds and mortgage backed securities, a policy dubbed QE, or "quantitative easing," there immediately arose many economic "experts" who predicted a significant increase in the price level, or even runaway inflation. In the period from 2009 to 2014, the Federal Reserve QE policy almost quadrupled the amount of reserves that banks have on deposit with Federal Reserve, resulting in a potentially huge increase in the money supply.

What has been the inflationary effect of QE? An article in the *Wall Street Journal* of January 29, 2009, written by J. Hilsenrath and L. Rappaport, indicated that, with regard to this QE plan, "some might see it … as an inflationary move to finance deficits by printing money." Yet six years later, despite the huge increase in the quantity of money stimulated by the Federal Reserve's QE policy, the rate of inflation in the United States is *less than* the 2 percent the Federal Reserve sees as a necessary inflationary price target if the economy is to perform strongly.

Keynes believed that money is never neutral and that changes in the quantity of money can affect the level of output and employment. He wrote:

> An economy which uses money but uses it merely as a *neutral* link between transactions in real things and real assets and does not allow it to enter into motives or decisions, might be called – for want of a better name – a *Real-Exchange Economy*. The theory which I desiderate would deal, in contradistinction to this, with an Economy in which Money plays a part on its own and affects motives and decisions and is, in short, one of the operative factors in the situation, so that the course of events cannot be predicted either in the long period or in the short, without a knowledge of the behavior of money between the first state and the last. And it is this which we ought to mean when we speak of a *Monetary Economy*. … Booms and depressions are peculiar to an economy in which money is not neutral. I believe that the next task is to work out in some detail such a monetary theory of production. That is

the task on which I am now occupying myself in some confidence that
I am not wasting my time.[14]

Once the neutrality of money is rejected as a necessary axiomatic
building block, then an organizing principle for studying the level
of employment and output in a market economy involves (1)
comprehending the role of money as a means of settling contractual
obligations and (2) understanding the essential role liquidity plays
in determining the flow of production and employment in the
economic system in which we live.

James K. Galbraith has noted that the first three words of the title
of Keynes's 1936 book *The General Theory of Employment,
Interest and Money* "are evidently cribbed from Albert Einstein."[15]
Einstein's general theory of relativity had displaced Newton's
classical theory in physics that had maintained the separation of
time and space. Einstein's demonstrated that the space–time continuum is, in essence, the extension of non-Euclidean Riemannian
geometry of curved spaces. Keynes hoped to mimic Einstein's
revolutionary general theory of relativity and displace the classical
economic theory that maintained the separation of market outcomes
and the money supply implied by the neutral money axiom. Keynes
wanted to replace this axiomatic separation with the equivalent of a
market money curved space continuum, that is, where money and
market outcomes continuously interact.

To accept Keynes's logic and its Post Keynesian development,
however, threatens the Panglossian conclusion that, in the long run,
all is for the best in this best of all possible worlds where an
unfettered market economy assures full employment and prosperity
for all those who want to work. The smaller axiomatic foundation
of Keynes's general theory allows for the possibility that an
entrepreneurial system might possess some inherent faults such as
its failure to provide for full employment even in the long run.
Keynes's logic is just as antithetical to the classical Social Darwin-
ist classical economic theory as the view on the origin of human
life as asserted by the "scientific theory of evolution" is to the
"intelligent design" view of some fundamentalist Christian reli-
gion's axiomatic belief in the biblical explanation of the creation of
human life.

Keynes's general theory suggests that this inability of the entrepreneurial system to provide full employment can be ameliorated

by developing corrective fiscal policies to assure sufficient market demand and regulatory institutions for stabilizing our financial markets, and not relying solely on monetary policies. *There can be a permanent role for government to correct systemic economic faults of the entrepreneurial system in which we live while preserving the freedom of entrepreneurial decision making and innovation.*

The Gross Substitution Axiom

The gross substitution axiom asserts that anything sold in the market is a gross substitute for anything else for sale in the market. This axiom means that a change in the relative price of any specific good or service will induce buyers to buy more of the item that is now cheaper and less of the items that have become more expensive while spending the same total amount of income. For example, if tea and coffee are gross substitutes then if the price of tea increases, people will buy less tea and purchase more coffee.

Arrow and Hahn[16] have demonstrated that if the gross substitution axiom is not universally applicable to all markets, then this jeopardizes all mathematical proofs that the system will achieve a Walrasian "general equilibrium" where there is full employment and all production is sold at a profit by firms. In other words, it cannot be proven that full employment will be an automatic outcome of free markets if the gross substitution axiom is not ubiquitously applied to all markets described in one's theory.

In a later chapter we will explain how Keynes's theory rejected the gross substitution axiom as applicable to producible things that savers use to store their savings to move the contractual purchasing power of savings to the indefinite future. We will see that in Keynes's theory of a money using economy, savers always store their savings in the form of money and/or other liquid financial assets. Savers never store their savings in producible goods, no matter what the relative price changes between producible goods and liquid assets. In other words, when Keynes described the process of savings he assumed that for storing savings over time, producible durable goods were not a gross substitute for storing savings in the form of liquid assets including money.[17] Thus the mere act of savings threatens the applicability of Say's Law since today's savings are not spent on buying today's products and services.[18]

NOTES

1. J. M. Keynes, *The General Theory of Employment, Interest and Money* (Macmillan, London, 1936) p. 383.
2. Op. cit., p. 372.
3. The term "objective" for the probability distribution is used to suggest it is created by natural parameters and cannot be altered by anything people decide to do today.
4. T. Sargent, *Bounded Rationality in Macroeconomics* (Clarendon Press, Oxford, 1993) p. 21.
5. Or its 19th-century perfect knowledge equivalent.
6. L. H. Summers and V. P. Summers, "When Financial Markets Work Too Well: A Cautious Case for a Securities Transaction Tax," *Journal of Financial Services, 3*, 1989, p. 166.
7. J. M. Keynes, Letter of 4 July 1938 to R. F. Harrod reprinted in *The Collected Writings of John Maynard Keynes, 14*, edited by D. Moggridge (Macmillan, London, 1973) pp. 112–115.
8. J. M. Keynes, "The General Theory of Employment," *Quarterly Journal of Economics, 51*, 1937, pp. 209–223, reprinted in *The Collected Writings of John Maynard Keynes, 14*, edited by D. Moggridge (Macmillan, London, 1973) pp. 113–114.
9. J. M. Keynes, "Mr. Tinbergen's Method," *Economic Journal* (1939), reprinted in *The Collected Writings of John Maynard Keynes, 14*, edited by D. Moggridge (Macmillan, London, 1973) p. 308.
10. J. R. Hicks, *Economic Perspectives* (Oxford Economic Press, Oxford, 1977) p. vii.
11. See, for example, P. A. Samuelson, "Classical and Neo Classical Theory," in *Monetary Theory*, edited by R. W. Clower (Penguin, London, 1969) pp. 104–105 and R. Lucas and T. Sargent, *Rational Expectations and Econometric Practices* (University of Minnesota Press, Minneapolis, MN, 1981) p. xii.
12. M. Friedman, "A Theoretical Framework for Monetary Analysis," in *Milton Friedman's Monetary Framework*, edited by R. J. Gordon (University of Chicago Press, Chicago, 1970) p. 27.
13. O. Blanchard, "Why Does Money Affect Output?" in *Handbook of Monetary Economics, 2*, edited by B. M. Friedman and F. H. Hahn (North Holland, New York, 1990) p. 828.
14. J. M. Keynes, "A Monetary Theory of Production," 1933, reprinted in *The Collected Writings of John Maynard Keynes, 13*, edited by D. Moggridge (MacMillan, London, 1973) pp. 408–411.
15. J. K. Galbraith, "Keynes, Einstein, and the Scientific Revolution," in *Keynes, Money and the Open Economy*, edited by P. Arestis (Edward Elgar, Cheltenham, UK and Brookfield, VT, 1996) p. 14.
16. K. J. Arrow and F. H. Hahn, *General Competitive Equilibrium* (Holden Day, San Francisco, CA, 1971) p. 361.
17. J. M. Keynes, *The General Theory*, pp. 231–232.
18. In the next chapter we will see that in order to restore Say's Law, Milton Friedman changed the definition of "savings" where all savings is defined as the purchase of newly produced durable goods. It may seem strange that the

purchase of a yacht or a mink coat is defined as savings by Friedman, but that is necessary to support the conclusions of Friedman's classical monetary theory.

4. Keynes–Post Keynesian theory: money and money contracts

The income principle behind Keynes's theory is simple. Income is earned whenever a person or firm sells a newly produced good or service in the market place. For example, when a person spends money to buy this book new, the total purchase price contributes to the income of the book seller, who, in turn, has paid part of this purchase price to contribute to the income of the publisher, who uses part to pay income to its employees. The publisher has paid a sum to the income of the printer for printing the book. Furthermore, the publisher contributes to the author's income by making a royalty payment equal to a contractual agreed upon percentage of the funds received from the book seller.

Whenever people decide to save part of their income instead of spending it on newly produced goods and services, that portion of income that is saved is denying other people income that would be earned if the saver had decided not to save, but rather to spend all of their income on newly produced goods and services.

In order for people and firms to earn income they must engage in the production of goods and services that someone else buys in the market place. Consequently, when workers cannot find employment, it is due to the fact that employers do not expect to be able to sell profitably the additional output that the unemployed workers, if hired, could help to produce. The cause of an economy being at less than full employment is a lack of sufficient market demand to encourage entrepreneurs to hire all the workers who are willing to work. Consequently, any government policy that is designed to reduce unemployment and move towards a more prosperous economy must be a policy that encourages additional market demand spending for the goods and services that can be produced by the domestic industries at full employment.

As we have already suggested, Say's Law specified that whenever more workers are hired to increase production (supply), there must be an equivalent increase in income, and *all* this additional income will be immediately spent on purchasing the additional production at a profitable market price. If, as Keynes claims, Say's Law is not a "true law," then the relevant theory has to explain why there can be a lack of sufficient market demand out of income to buy all the things that a fully employed economy can produce.

In developing his general theory, it became obvious to Keynes that the classical conception of savings was a vague notion that meant different things in different contexts. Under the influence of the philosopher G. E. Moore,[1] Keynes recognized that a precise taxonomy regarding classification of events in economics, like in biology, is crucial to scientific structure. As Keynes's first biographer, Roy Harrod, noted: "The real defect with the classical system was that it deflected attention from what most needed attention. It was Keynes' extraordinary powerful intuitive sense of what was important that convinced him the old classification system was inadequate."[2]

Consequently, it was necessary to develop precise definitions regarding different categories of spending out of current income in order to analyze and understand the cause of unemployment in the economic system. Keynes's explanation of why there could be a lack of sufficient aggregate market demand for all the goods and services that could be produced at full employment depended on providing a precise definition of savings out of current income – a definition that was different to that required by classical theory.

Keynes defined consumption as that portion of income used to buy producible goods currently. He defined savings as that portion of current money income that is not used currently to buy goods and services. Or, as Keynes put it, "An act of individual savings means – so to speak – a decision not to have dinner to-day. But it does *not* necessitate a decision to have dinner or buy a pair of boots a week hence or a year hence or to consume any specified thing at any specified date. Thus it depresses the business of preparing to-day's dinner without stimulating the business of making ready for some future act of consumption."[3]

Keynes then noted that in a monetary economy savers store their savings out of current income in the form of money (currency and bank deposits) and/or any other liquid assets that can be readily sold in some financial market to obtain money. Why are money and liquid assets so important as the only things used to store current savings?

In their book entitled *General Competitive Equilibrium*, Arrow and Hahn wrote:

> The terms in which contracts are made matter. In particular, if money is the goods in terms of which contracts are made, then the prices of goods in terms of money are of special significance. This is not the case if we consider an economy without a past or future. ... *if a serious monetary theory* comes to be written, the fact that contracts are made in terms of money will be of considerable importance.[4]

Classical theory, on the other hand, presumed that a decision to save was equivalent to a decision to order to purchase a specific producible good or service at a specific date in the future. Savings was merely what Classical Theorists called a "time preference" ordering of what goods to buy out of all one's income at each point of time. Thus in classical theory, all income was spent as decision makers enter into real contracts, not money contracts, for the purchase and sale of specific goods and services[5] either for delivery today or a specific date in the future.

If Arrow and Hahn are correct, then the classical mainstream theories that presumed all contracts were real contracts, whether they be developed from static classical Walrasian theories, dynamic general equilibrium systems or even mainstream "Keynesian" theories, do not, and cannot, provide the foundation for "a serious monetary theory."

Keynes's liquidity theory of employment, and its development by Post Keynesians, however, develops a "serious monetary theory" for all domestic and international market transactions. This theory emphasizes that all market transactions involving production and exchanges in a modern market oriented economy are organized via the use of money denominated contracts.

Why money contracts? Keynes emphasized the use of money contracts as an important way decision makers could deal with the problem of uncertainty about the future outcomes of today's decisions in our economic system. This money contracting view provides a new way of economic thinking to explain the operations of a monetary economy where entrepreneurs and households enter into money denominated contracts in order to deal with the uncertain future.

We live in an economy with an irrevocable past and an uncertain future. In this world, decision makers know that they do not, and cannot, with any degree of certainty know the real economic future. Yet they must live with decisions made today whose real outcome can only be known in the future. Accordingly, the capitalist system has developed the institution of legal money contracts that are used to organize *all* market production and exchange transactions. The use of money contracts provides buyer and seller decision makers with at least some legal contractual certainty and control over future cash inflows and outflows resulting from today's economic decisions. Money contracts over time produce the liquidity concept for individuals that involves the ability to meet one's money contractual obligations as they come due. This liquidity concept is an essential aspect of market decision making in a capitalist economy with a financial market system. The need for liquidity affects economic motives and decisions in the market place.

The sanctity of money contracts is the essence of the capitalist system and *Keynes's analysis.* Keynes's theory is, in the Arrow–Hahn terminology, *a serious monetary theory.* In the Keynes–Post Keynesian theory, liquidity, that is, the ability to meet one's money contractual commitments domestically and internationally, becomes an essential foundation for understanding what affects motives and decisions in entering into transaction contractual agreements in the operation of an entrepreneurial, market oriented, money using economy.

Under the civil law of contracts, money is the thing that a government decides will settle all legal contractual obligations. Since the government makes and enforces the legal system, all law abiding citizens find their need for liquidity typically takes the form of maintaining a positive balance in their bank deposit checkbook and currency in their wallets so all contractual obligations can be met as they come due. If, at any time, one's bank deposit is close to being overdrawn, the typical solution is to:

1.   stop entering into additional money contractual payment obligations until more of one's cash inflow is received to increase one's deposit into one's bank account;

2.   arrange for a bank line of credit; or
3.   sell a liquid financial asset and use the money to replenish one's bank account.

Since the future is uncertain, individual decision makers never know when they might be suddenly faced with a money contractual payment obligation at a future date that they did not, or could not, anticipate and/or that they cannot meet out of the cash inflows expected at that future date. Decision makers never know if an expected cash inflow will suddenly disappear for any unexpected reason – for example, a reduction in pension income due to financial market value declines, or a loss of job, or the death of the breadwinner in the family, or a government austerity program that impacts the decision maker's cash inflow, or an asset that was held in one's portfolio that was thought to be liquid (could easily be sold for money) – such as mortgage backed derivatives – but suddenly becomes illiquid and therefore cannot be readily sold for money.

Accordingly, there is a precautionary liquidity motive for maintaining a positive bank deposit balance in order to protect against any unforeseen cash flow problems. *In our society, no one can either be too handsome, or too beautiful or too liquid.* As long as the future is uncertain, enhancing one's liquidity position will cushion the blow of any contractual obligations that may occur. The more one fears the economic uncertain future, the bigger liquidity security cushion is desirable. Savings out of current income are always (and only) stored in the form of money or other durable liquid assets that are not costly to hold and can be readily and inexpensively converted into money to meet any future contractual obligations.

In the very beginning of his *Treatise on Money*, Keynes wrote that money

> comes into existence along with Debts, which are contracts for deferred payments, and Price-Lists, which are offers of contracts for sale or purchase. ... Money itself, [is] namely that by delivery of which debt-contracts and price-contracts are *discharged*, and in the shape of which a store of General Purchasing Power is held. ... Furthermore it is a peculiar characteristic of money contracts that it is the State or community not only which enforces delivery, but also which decides what it is that must be delivered as a lawful ... discharge of a contract ... . And the Age of Chartalist or State Money was reached when the

State claimed the right to declare what thing should answer as money ... when it claimed the right not only to enforce the dictionary but also to write the dictionary. To-day all civilised money is, beyond the possibility of dispute, Chartalist.[6]

What distinguishes the Keynes–Post Keynesian analysis from classical mainstream macroeconomic theory involves an analysis of whether decision makers can know with certainty the economic future involving real or money payouts and economic events in the uncertain future. In most orthodox equilibrium analysis, it is presumed decision makers know the future or, at least, have rational expectations about the future that provide actuarially correct knowledge about the future.

Keynes and his Post Keynesian followers[7] all reject the ergodic axiom or any other assumption that presumes people can "know" the economic future. The rationale for such a rejection is that the economic future is not predetermined; rather it will be created by people's expectations, motivations and liquidity behavior in the market place. Keynes and the Post Keynesians insist that people "know" they cannot know the future outcome of crucial economic decisions made today. The future is truly uncertain and not just probabilistically risky.

The Keynes liquidity theory and George Soros's concept of reflexivity both reject the ergodic axiom. This alternative to the classical theory assumes a nonergodic environment; yet, it still provides one with a scientific understanding of the operation and functioning of financial markets in a capitalist system. *The primary function of all well-organized and orderly financial markets is to provide liquidity* so that holders of financial assets traded on such orderly markets "know" they can make a *fast exit* from their liquid financial asset portfolio by selling securities for money at a price close to the previous price in the market. For business firms and households, the maintenance of one's liquid position to meet all possible future contractual obligations is of prime importance if bankruptcy is to be avoided. In our world, bankruptcy is the economic equivalent to a walk to the gallows.

SAVINGS AND LIQUIDITY

Saving is the attempt of savers to put some of today's cash inflow that is not spent to buy goods and services into some low carrying cost time-machine to carry the contractual settlement (purchasing) power of this cash money inflow into the indefinite future. This time-machine function is known as *liquidity*. The possession of liquidity means that the person has sufficient money (or other liquid assets that can be readily resold for money in an orderly, organized market) to meet all his/her contractual obligations as they come due. In a world of uncertainty, a decision maker cannot know what contracts either already entered into, or which will be entered into in the future, will be defaulted by the payer when the decision maker is the pay recipient. The decision maker also does not know if there will be a need for more money for him/her to discharge all future contractual obligations as they come due.

Money is the liquid asset par excellence, for it can always settle any contractual obligation as long as the residents of the economy are law abiding and recognize the civil law of contracts. The more uncertain the decision maker feels about future economic events, the more money (or liquidity) he/she will desire to hold to meet possible unforeseen money contract contingencies. This characteristic of liquidity can be possessed in various degrees by some, but not all, possible durables. Since any durable besides money can*not* (by definition) settle a contract, then for durables other than money to be a liquidity time-machine they must have (1) low carrying costs and (2) low sales transaction costs by being easily salable in well-organized, orderly markets for money.[8]

The market for liquid financial assets must be well organized so as to have low transaction costs in bringing buyers and sellers together. The market also must be orderly, that is, any change in the market price from minute to minute must move in an orderly manner so that the next transaction price is not very different from the previous transaction price. As long as the market is orderly, the holder of market securities believes he/she can make a fast exit at a price not much different than the previously publically announced price.

The necessary condition for any market to be well organized and orderly is that there must be a market maker, that is, an institution possessing sufficient resources that it can and will make the market when there is a sudden absence of sufficient buyers (bulls) or sellers (bears). The market maker does not necessarily guarantee that the market price will never change over time. The market maker need only assure market participants that if the market price does change, it will change in an orderly manner, given the explicit, known rules under which the market maker operates.

For any liquid security asset the next moment's market price is never known with certainty. What is known is that the price will not move in a disorderly manner from the last prices because the market maker has sufficient liquidity to back up his/her assurance of an orderly market. For example, if suddenly many private sector holders of a specific financial asset turn bearish and try to make a fast exit from the market by selling their portfolio holdings, and there are not enough bulls to allow the bears to make an orderly exit from the financial market, then the market maker steps in and buys to maintain price movement orderliness in the market. If this private sector market maker's own resources are insufficient to maintain orderliness when there is a "herd behavior" rush to the exit, then trading is usually suspended via circuit breakers until the market maker can obtain sufficient resources to maintain orderliness and/or the panic subsides. If the private sector market maker cannot restore order in an important financial market, then it is the central banker who may have to become the *market maker of last resort* to either directly, or through providing resources to the market maker, restore orderliness.

A *fully liquid asset* is defined as any financial asset traded in a market where the private sector participants in the market "know" that the market price in terms of monetary units will not change for the foreseeable future. To be a fully liquid asset, there must be a market maker who can guarantee that the money price of the asset will not change over time even if circumstances change. An example of a fully liquid asset is a foreign currency whose value in terms of domestic currency is fixed by the central bank of the nation. (As long as the central bank has sufficient foreign reserves, it can, if it wishes, guarantee a fixed exchange rate.)

A *liquid asset* is a durable asset readily resalable in a well-organized market, but the market maker does not guarantee an unchanging market price. The market maker only assures market prices will change in an orderly manner.

An *illiquid asset* is an asset that cannot be readily resalable at any price in the market. Illiquid assets do not have orderly, organized resale markets. There is no market maker who is willing to organize an orderly market for the illiquid asset.

ESSENTIAL PROPERTIES OF LIQUID ASSETS

As Keynes developed his theory of liquidity preference he recognized that his theory of involuntary unemployment required devoting an entire chapter of his book to, the chapter being titled "The Essential Properties of Interest and Money."[9] These essential properties that are characteristic of all liquid assets are the basis for differentiating Keynes's explanation of unemployment from the classical theory's explanation that blames noncompetitive markets that reflect fixities in money wages and product prices. Keynes stated: "the Classical Theory has been accustomed to rest the supposedly self-adjusting character of the economic system on an assumed fluidity of money-wages; and, where there is a rigidity, to lay on this rigidity the blame for maladjustment. … My difference from this theory is primarily a difference of analysis."[10]

To explain unemployment due to a lack of sufficient market demand, Keynes identified two essential properties of money and all other liquid assets. Keynes stated: "The attribute of 'liquidity' is by no means independent of the presence of these two characteristics."[11] These two essential properties of all liquid assets are:

1. the elasticity of production of all liquid assets including money is zero or negligible;
2. the elasticity of substitution between liquid assets (including money) and reproducible goods is zero or negligible.

A zero elasticity of production means that money does not grow on trees and consequently workers cannot be hired by private sector entrepreneurs to harvest money trees when the demand for money (liquidity) increases. Or, as Keynes wrote, "money … cannot be readily reproduced; – labour cannot be turned on at will by entrepreneurs to produce money in increasing quantities as its price rises."[12] In other words, when the demand for money (liquidity) increases, private sector entrepreneurs cannot hire labor to produce more money to meet this increase in demand for these nonreproducible (by workers in the private sector) liquid assets.

The second "essential property" is a zero elasticity of substitution. In Keynes's theory, savings are defined as any portion of currently earned income that is not spent on currently produced goods and services. In Keynes's analysis, all savings are held either in the form of money or other liquid assets. A zero elasticity of substitution assures that the savings portion of income is not spent on producible goods and services. Instead, savings are stored in what Frank Hahn[13] called nonproducible "resting places." For Keynes, liquid assets are the "resting places" for savings. When people add to their savings and therefore increase the demand for liquid assets, the price of liquid assets will increase. If the elasticity of substitution is zero, the increase in the prices of these nonproducibles will not induce savers to substitute producibles for these nonproducible liquid assets as a store for their savings.

In his 1977 paper, Hahn rediscovered Keynes's point that a stable involuntary unemployment equilibrium could exist *even in a purely competitive system with flexible wages and prices* of producible goods and services whenever there are "resting places for savings in other than reproducible assets."[14] Hahn rigorously demonstrated what was logically intuitive to Keynes. Hahn showed that the view that with "flexible money wages there would be no unemployment has no convincing argument to recommend it … . Even in a pure tatonnement in traditional models convergence to [a general] equilibrium cannot be generally proved"[15] if savings were held in the form of nonproducibles. Hahn argued that "any non-reproducible asset allows for a choice between employment inducing and non-employment inducing demand."[16] If a portion of income earned in producing goods and services is saved to be used to demand nonproducible liquid assets, then Say's Law is no longer applicable no matter how flexible wages and prices of producibles are. By definition, Say's Law requires that all income earned in the production of producibles must be spent on the demand for producibles.

Accordingly, if income earning savers store their savings in money and other liquid nonreproducible assets (that are *not* gross substitutes for the products of the capital goods producing industries), then all income earned by households engaging in the production of goods in any period is not, in the short or long run, necessarily spent on the products of industry. Households who want to store that portion of their income they do not consume (i.e., that they do not spend on the products of industry) in liquid assets are choosing, in Hahn's words, "a non-employment inducing demand" for their savings.

Apparently, Milton Friedman recognized this conceptualization of savings stored in the form of nonproducibles as a problem for classical theory and the monetary economic analysis that he championed. Accordingly, in his theory, Friedman implicitly resurrected the applicability of Say's Law for his analysis when he redefined the fact of what is "savings" to terms that must seem strange to most intelligent people. For Friedman, savings out of current income receipts are defined as being used to demand in the market some producible durables that are purchased today but are not immediately entirely consumed in the same day. Friedman does this by redefining consumption as "the value of services consumed" (utility) during each accounting period.[17] Since, by definition, a durable good will last for more than one day or accounting period, the total services derived from any produced durable cannot be consumed all in the one day of purchase. Consumption is therefore defined by Friedman as the purchase of all nondurables during the accounting period plus the depreciation or wearing out of any possessed durables during the same period. Thus, in Friedman's theory of a monetary economy, the purchase of long-lived producible durables, such as cars, appliances, a diamond ring, a yacht, a private airplane and so on, in the current period is defined as savings out of current income (except for the slight depreciation during the current period).

Friedman claims this taxonomy is superior to others because "much that one classifies as consumption is reclassified as savings."[18] Accordingly, Friedman can still maintain the axiom of the neutrality of money by redefining what people call savings. This new Friedman taxonomy suggests that the "facts" regarding what most people think as savings in the form of liquid assets that might support the Keynes analysis are wrong. When these "facts" about savings are redefined, then, in Friedman's model, the savings by households create jobs just as much as household spending on nondurable consumption goods like food does. Friedman's taxonomy implicitly reintroduces Say's Law into his economic model – as now all income whether it is saved or spent on consumption will be spent on the purchase of newly produced goods and services. Which definition of savings does the reader believe is more realistic: Friedman's, where a purchase of a new yacht is still defined as savings, or Keynes's, where the purchase of a yacht for pleasure boating is called consumption (or even conspicuous consumption by some)?

According to Keynes, as long as savers store their savings in liquid assets that have zero or "low elasticity of production and substitution,"[19] then involuntary unemployment equilibrium is possible even in the long run in an economic system with flexible wages and prices. Consequently, Say's Law is never applicable in such a monetary liquidity system. Keynes's serious monetary theory of liquidity explains possible involuntary unemployment as the result of savings finding resting places in nonproducible liquid assets where the desired level of savings by savers is not offset by equal dissavings of others in the same accounting period. Accordingly, whenever there is a significant strong aggregate propensity to save by savers in the form of liquid assets in the macroeconomy, there must be other decision makers willing to spend enough to dissave (go into debt?) if the economy is not to fall into recession.

Clearly, the differing definition of savings and the lack of any concept of liquidity in the Friedman classical model imply no need for the government deficit spending to assure full employment since, under Friedman's redefinition of the facts, Say's Law will provide full employment. The Keynes (and Hahn) analysis provides a differing rationale for the role of government policies that should be aimed at encouraging dissavings in the system to offset aggregate savings in order to end recessionary pressures in a modern economy.

NOTES

1. G. E. Moore, *Principia Ethica* (Cambridge University Press, Cambridge, 1903).
2. R. F. Harrod, *The Life of John Maynard Keynes* (Macmillan, London, 1951) pp. 463–464.
3. J. M. Keynes, *The General Theory of Employment, Interest and Money* (Macmillan, London, 1936) p. 210.
4. K. J. Arrow and F. H. Hahn, *General Competitive Equilibrium* (Holden Day, San Francisco, CA, 1971) pp. 256–257, emphasis added.

5. A real contract, however, is one where any money payment is adjusted for any inflation that may have occurred between the time the contract is agreed upon and the time when payment must be made. In our economic world, an example of a real contract occurred when, in the 1970s, automobile manufacturers accepted union contracts that included a cost of living adjustment (COLA) clause. The contractual COLA clause specified that workers were to be paid each month a basic money wage that would be adjusted for the rate of inflation experienced in the previous month. For example, if the basic money wage specified in the contract was $100 per week and the economy experienced a 3 percent rate of inflation last month, then the money wage paid to workers this month would be $103 per week. In essence, the contract required payment in what economists term "real" wages.
6. J. M. Keynes, *A Treatise on Money, 1* (MacMillan, London, 1930) pp. 3–4.
7. And even George Soros, "Letter to the Editor," *The Economist*, March 15–21, 1997 issue.
8. Even if an organized resale market exists for producible durable goods, these durable producibles typically have high carrying costs and high resale costs compared to money and other liquid financial assets. Accordingly, producible durable goods are not the things in which people tend to store their savings. For example, despite a market for second hand automobiles, savers do not store their savings out of current income via the purchase of an automobile.
9. J. M. Keynes, *The General Theory of Employment, Interest and Money* (Macmillan, London, 1936) Chapter 17.
10. Op. cit., p. 257.
11. Op. cit., p. 241 n. 1.
12. Op cit., p. 230.
13. F. H. Hahn, "Keynesian Economics and General Equilibrium Theory," in *The Microeconomic Foundations of Macroeconomics*, edited by G. C. Harcourt (Macmillan, London, 1977) p. 31.
14. Op. cit., p. 31.
15. Op. cit., p. 37.
16. Op cit., p. 39.
17. M. Friedman, *The Theory of Permanent Income* (Princeton University Press, Princeton, NJ, 1957) p. 11.
18. Op. cit., p. 28.
19. J. M. Keynes, *The General Theory*, p. 238.

5. Why traditional mainstream Keynesian theory is not Keynes's theory

Long before Keynes developed his general theory to explain why persistent unemployment could occur in the economy, classical theory had explained unemployment as the result of short-term imperfections or monopoly elements on the supply side of the market system. These imperfections took the form of rigidities in the market money wage rate and/or product prices due to noncompetitive labor and product markets. If there was no government interference during these periods of unemployment, then the resulting weakened markets would induce sufficient competition to make wages and prices more flexible in a downward direction and would ultimately weed out the imperfections leaving a stronger, more powerful full employment economy to carry on.

In essence, classical theory suggested that unemployment and depressions were merely the working of nature's law of the jungle. Ultimately, the market would solve the problem by inducing a competitive economic environment that, in Darwinian fashion, would kill off the weak and inefficient, thereby assuring the survival of the fittest. When the economy purged itself of its imperfections, it would generate full employment and prosperity for all the survivors.

An example of how this classical economic theory affected government decision making is provided in the autobiography of President Herbert Hoover, who was president of the United States when the Great Depression began in 1929. Hoover indicates that whenever he wanted to take some positive action to end the depression, his Treasury Secretary, Andrew Mellon, always cautioned against government action and gave the same advice. Hoover wrote: "Mr. Mellon had only one formula. Liquidate labor, liquidate stocks, liquidate the farmer, liquidate real estate. It will purge the rottenness out of the system. ... People will work harder, lead a moral life."[1]

As we have noted in previous chapters, Keynes's general theory indicated that it was not the monopoly elements in the labor and product markets that were the prime cause of unemployment and economic depression. The prime cause was too much savings in the form of liquid assets relative to decisions to spend on goods and services. Keynes explicitly demonstrated that even in a competitive economy where wages and prices are perfectly flexible, persistent unemployment can, and often would, occur.[2]

Nevertheless, the development of what was called "Keynesianism" in the United States and other nations after the Second World War was based on the same classical axioms that Keynes had overthrown in developing his general theory alternative to classical theory. This failure of immediate post war so-called Keynesian theory to follow Keynes's general theory was the result of Nobel Prize Laureate Paul Samuelson's domination of economists' thinking in all nations about what Samuelson thought was the basis of Keynes's revolution in economic thought.

Paul Samuelson was the founder of the American Keynesian school, which he labeled "neoclassical synthesis Keynesianism" because of the classical Walrasian microeconomic theory that Samuelson believed, and insisted, was the foundation of all economic theory including Keynes's macroeconomic theory. Samuelson's most famous introductory economics textbook, *Economics: An Introductory Analysis*, first published in 1948, has gone through 19 editions and is the most widely sold economics text ever (over 4 million copies). In the more than half century since Samuelson published his textbook, most economists (and politicians) got their first exposure to what was called "Keynesianism" from Samuelson or one of his New Keynesian textbook followers. It should not be a surprise, therefore, to see that mainstream economists around the globe believe that Post Keynesian theory does not fit into this Samuelson description of a valid economic analysis.

In 1941, Samuelson's Ph. D. dissertation won the Wells prize for the best Ph. D. dissertation in economics at Harvard. Thus, at the very beginning of his career as an economist, Samuelson was already identified by the classical economic theorists' establishment of that day at Harvard as one of its upcoming great analysts. Samuelson's dissertation was polished and finally published as

Foundations of Economic Analysis.[3] Based on Samuelson's view of what was the foundation of all economic theory, any branch of mainstream Keynesianism – for example, neoclassical synthesis Keynesianism and New Keynesianism – had to build on a classical microeconomic Walrasian general equilibrium foundation. If the microfoundations of any macroeconomics theory was not Walrasian, then, according to Samuelson, such a theory could neither be what Keynes meant nor a valid theory of macroeconomics.

Paul Samuelson claimed that his Ph. D. dissertation had discovered, understood, explained and published in mathematical form the only possible microfoundations of *all* economic theory, including Keynes's general theory. When Samuelson produced a textbook simplification of what he believed was Keynes's theory, this encouraged mainstream economists to not even try to read Keynes's *General Theory* book and its explanation of the "essential properties" of liquid assets as the fundamental cause of unemployment.

In their book, *The Coming of Keynesianism to America*, Colander and Landreth[4] credit Paul Samuelson with saving the textbook pedagogical basis of the Keynesian Revolution from destruction by the anti-communist spirit (McCarthyism) that ravaged America in the years immediately following the Second World War.

Lorie Tarshis, a Canadian who had been a student attending Keynes's lectures at Cambridge during the early 1930s, had, in 1947, published an introductory textbook[5] that incorporated Tarshis's lecture notes as his interpretation of Keynes's *General Theory*. Colander and Landreth noted that despite the initial popularity of the Tarshis textbook, its sales declined rapidly as it was attacked by trustees of, and donors to, American colleges and universities as preaching a "socialist" economic heresy. The frenzy about Tarshis's textbook reached a pinnacle when in 1951 William Buckley, in his book *God and Man at Yale*,[6] attacked the Tarshis analysis as communist inspired.

In August 1986 Colander and Landreth (hereafter C–L) interviewed Paul Samuelson about his becoming an economist and a "Keynesian."[7] Samuelson indicated that he recognized the "virulence of the attack on Tarshis" and so he wrote his textbook "carefully and lawyer like."[8] The term "neoclassical synthesis Keynesianism" did not appear in the first edition of Samuelson's textbook, *Economics: An Introductory Analysis*,[9] which was published just as the attack on Tarshis's textbook was growing. This neoclassical synthesis terminology, however, does appears prominently in the later editions of Samuelson's textbook. From hindsight, it would appear that Samuelson's pronounced assertion that his brand of Keynesian macroeconomics is synthesized with (and based on) traditional neoclassical Walrasian theory made the Samuelson version of Keynesianism less open to attacks of bringing socialist economic heresy into university courses on economics.

Samuelson proclaimed the need for a Walrasian foundation for all economic theories despite the fact that Keynes, as a student of Alfred Marshall (who was a famous economist in his own right), had based *The General Theory*'s microfoundations on Marshall's microeconomic analysis and not Walrasian classical analysis. Moreover, Keynes had denounced Walras's theory as wrong when he wrote "Now the analysis of the previous chapters [of *The General Theory*] made it plain that this account [in Walras] of the matter must be erroneous ... this [Walrasian system] is a nonsense theory."[10] Samuelson still claimed that Keynes's analysis must be based on the rigidity of wages and prices in a Walrasian system despite Keynes's statement that Walras's analysis is a "nonsense theory."

In his 1986 interview with C–L, Samuelson indicated that in the period before the Second World War, "my friends who were not economists regarded me as very conservative."[11] Samuelson graduated from the University of Chicago in June 1935, and, as he explained to C–L, were it not for the Social Science Research Council fellowship that he received upon graduation, he would have done his graduate studies at the University of Chicago[12] where even today the faculty of the economics department is one of the strongest defenders of classical theory. Consequently, it was the visible hand of a fellowship offer that placed Samuelson at Harvard when Keynes's *General Theory* was published in 1936. So one might ask what information about Keynes's *General Theory* was Samuelson exposed to at Harvard?

Robert Bryce, a Canadian, had attended Keynes's Cambridge lectures between 1932 and 1935. In a 1987 interview with C–L,[13] Bryce indicated that in the spring of 1935 he (Bryce) spent half of each week at LSE and half at Cambridge. At LSE, Bryce used his Cambridge lecture notes to write an essay on Keynes's revolutionary ideas – without having read *The General Theory*. This essay so impressed the champion Austrian classical economics professor

Frederick Hayek that Hayek let Bryce have four consecutive weeks of Hayek's seminar to explain Keynes's ideas as Bryce had written them out in this essay. Bryce's lectures were a huge success at the LSE.[14]

In the fall of 1935, Bryce went to Harvard and stayed for two years. During that time, an informal group met during the evenings to discuss Keynes's book. Bryce, using the same pre- *General Theory* essay that he had used as the basis for his talks at the LSE, presented to this group what he believed was Keynes's *General Theory* analysis – although he still had not read Keynes's *General Theory*. So, in 1936, the information in Bryce's essay became the basis of what most economists at Harvard, including Samuelson, thought was Keynes's analysis.

Even in 1987, Bryce said about Keynes's *General Theory* book that "anyone who studies that book is going to get very confused. It was … a difficult, provocative book."[15] The immediate question therefore is: Did Bryce ever really comprehend the basis of Keynes's analytical framework? If he did not, how did that affect how the young Samuelson and others at Harvard in 1936 learned about Keynes's analytical framework?

Samuelson has indicated that his first knowledge of Keynes's *General Theory* was gained from Bryce.[16] Moreover, even after reading *The General Theory* in 1936, Samuelson, perhaps reflecting Bryce's view of the difficulty of understanding Keynes's book, found the *General Theory*'s analysis "unpalatable" and not comprehensible.[17] Samuelson finally indicated that

> The way I finally convinced myself was to just stop worrying about it [about understanding Keynes's analysis]. I asked myself: why do I refuse a paradigm that enables me to understand the Roosevelt upturn from 1933 till 1937? … *I was content to assume that there was enough rigidity in relative prices and wages to make the Keynesian alternative to Walras operative.*[18]

It is apparent from Samuelson's writings that he believed that if Walrasian classical theory were the correct theory applicable to our monetary, market oriented economy, then this Walrasian system would, in fact, be the "general theory." Samuelson's view that Keynes's theory merely involved the assumption of rigidity of wages in an otherwise Walrasian system would then become a

special case of the general theory of Walrasian economics. It is
worth noting that, following Samuelson's lead, mainstream economists after the Second World War treated Keynes's theory as a
"special case" of the classical (Walrasian) general theory, applicable
only to conditions where money wages, and prices, were sticky and
even interest rates could become "sticky."

Apparently, Samuelson never tried to comprehend Keynes's
Marshallian analytical foundation and framework. For in 1986
Samuelson was still claiming that "we [Keynesians] always
assumed that the Keynesian underemployment equilibrium floated
on a substructure of administered prices and imperfect competition."[19] When pushed by C–L as to whether this requirement of
price and wage rigidity was ever formalized in his work, Samuelson's response was, "There was no need to."[20]

Yet specifically in Chapter 19 of *The General Theory*, entitled
"Changes in Money Wages," and even more directly in Keynes's
published response to an article published by Dunlop,[21] Keynes had
already responded in the negative to this question of whether his
analysis of the cause of unemployment equilibrium required imperfect competition, administered prices and/or rigid wages.[22] Dunlop
had argued that the purely competitive model was not empirically
justified, therefore it was monopolistic price and wage fixities that
must be the basis of Keynes's unemployment equilibrium. Keynes
reply was simply: "I complain a little that I in particular should be
criticised for conceding a little to the other view."[23] In chapters
17–19 of his *General Theory*, Keynes explicitly demonstrated that
even if perfectly flexible money wages and prices existed ("conceding a little to the other side"), there would be no automatic market
mechanism that could restore the full employment level of effective
demand. In other words, Keynes's general theory – using Marshallian microfoundations – could show that, as a matter of logic, less
than full employment equilibrium could exist in a purely competitive economy with freely flexible wages and prices.

It is difficult to understand why Samuelson, who became the
premier Keynesian of his time, never mentioned or recognized (1)
Keynes's response to Dunlop or even (2) Chapter 19 of *The
General Theory*, which was entitled "Changes in Money Wages." In
Chapter 19 Keynes explicitly indicates that the theory of unemploy-
ment equilibrium did not require "a rigidity" in money wages. As
Keynes put it:

For the classical theory has been so accustomed to rest the supposedly self-adjusting character of the economic system on the assumed fluidity of money wages; and, when there is rigidity, to lay on this rigidity the blame of maladjustment. ... My difference from this theory is primarily a difference of analysis.[24]

Keynes indicated that to assume that rigidity was *the* sole cause of the existence of an unemployment equilibrium lay in accepting the argument that the micro-demand functions "can only be constructed on some fixed assumption as to the nature of the demand and supply schedules of other industries and fixity as to the amount of aggregate effective demand."[25] It is invalid, therefore, to transfer the argument to industry as a whole unless we also transfer the argument that the total effective market demand is fixed. Yet, Keynes argued this assumption reduces the argument to "an *ignoratio elenchi*."[26]

An *ignoratio elenchi* is a fallacy in the logic of offering a proof irrelevant to the proposition in question. Unfortunately, Samuelson invoked the same classical *ignoratio elenchi* when he argued that Keynes's general theory was simply a Walrasian general equilibrium system where, in the short run, if there was an exogenous shock to effective demand, rigid wages and prices created a market force that created a temporary period of unemployment. In the long run, aggregate market demand was sufficient so that with flexible money wages full employment would be restored as the money wage declined.

As Keynes went on to explain,

whilst no one would wish to deny the proposition that a reduction in money wages *accompanied by the same aggregate effective [market] demand as before* will be associated with an increase in employment, the precise question at issue is whether the reduction in money-wages will or will not be accompanied by the same aggregate effective demand as before measured in term of money, or, at any rate, by an aggregate effective demand which is not reduced in full proportion to the reduction in money-wages.[27]

Keynes then spent the rest of Chapter 19 explaining why and how a general theory analysis must look at the relationship between changes in money wages and/or prices and changes in aggregate effective market demand[28] – an analysis that, by assumption, is not relevant to either a Walrasian system or Samuelson's neoclassical synthesis Keynesianism.

At the same time that Samuelson became a Keynesian, believing in Walrasian foundations for all economic theory, by convincing himself not to worry about Keynes's actual analytical framework, Tarshis had obtained a position at Tufts University, a mere half-hour of travel from Harvard. Tarshis would often meet with the group at Harvard, including Bryce, who were discussing Keynes. Tarshis notes that "Paul Samuelson was not in the Keynesian group. He was busy working on his own thing. That he became a Keynesian was laughable."[29] Yet, Paul Samuelson has called himself a "Keynesian" and even a "Post Keynesian" in several editions of his famous textbook. Nevertheless, Samuelson's theoretical "neoclassical synthesis" axiomatic foundations logically is not the general theory spelled out by Keynes.

At the same time that Samuelson was developing his neoclassical synthesis Keynesianism, he was working on cleaning up his 1947 book *Foundations of Economic Analysis*. In his *Foundations* book Samuelson asserts certain specific classical axiom foundations that are the basis of classical theory and, therefore, his neoclassical Keynesian macroeconomic analysis. For example, Samuelson noted that "in a purely competitive world it would be foolish to hold money as a store of value as long as other assets had a positive yield."[30] This statement means that (1) any real producible capital goods that produce a positive yield must be gross substitutes for money as a form to hold one's savings and (2) money is neutral. Thus, at the same time Samuelson was promoting his pedagogical brand of Keynesianism in his textbook he was arguing that the gross substitution axiom and the neutral money axiom are part of the foundations upon which all economic analysis must be built. Yet, as we have already noted, Keynes explicitly rejected these two classical axioms as a foundation for his general theory.

Furthermore, in an article published in 1969, Samuelson argued that the "ergodic hypothesis [axiom]" is a necessary foundation if economics is to be a "hard science."[31] (As we have already explained, Keynes had also rejected this ergodic axiom.)

Samuelson has stated that in his view Keynes's analysis is a "very slow adjusting disequilibrium" system where the "full Walrasian equilibrium was not realized" in the short run because prices and wages do not adjust rapidly enough to an exogenous shock.[32]

Nevertheless, the economic system would, if left alone, achieve full employment in the long run.

In contrast, on the first text page of *The General Theory*, Keynes explained that the

> postulates of the classical [Walrasian] theory are applicable to a special case only and not to the general case ... . Moreover the characteristics of the special case assumed by the classical theory happen not to be those of the economics society in which we actually live, with the result that its teaching is misleading and disastrous if we attempt to apply it to the facts of experience.[33]

In the preface to the German language edition of *The General Theory*, Keynes specifically noted, "This is one of the reasons which justify my calling my theory a *general* theory. Since it is *based on fewer restrictive assumptions* ["weniger enge Voraussetzunger stutz"] than the orthodox theory, it is also more easily adopted to a large area of different circumstances."[34] In other words, Keynes argued that what made his analytical system more general than the classical (or Walrasian general equilibrium) analysis is that his general theory requires a smaller axiomatic base (fewer restrictive axioms) than Walrasian theory. Alternative theories such as the Walrasian approach then are special cases that impose additional restrictive axioms to the common smaller axiomatic foundation of Keynes's general theory. The onus is, therefore, on those like Samuelson who add restrictive axioms to the general theory to justify these additional axioms. Those theorists who invoke only the general theory's smaller axiomatic base are not required, in logic, to prove a general negative; that is, they are not required to prove the additional restrictive axioms are unnecessary.

Sidney Weintraub, a founder of Post Keynesian theory, developed Keynes's principle of effective demand by utilizing Alfred Marshall's microeconomic theory approach. Weintraub demonstrated that Keynes's aggregate supply function could be derived from Marshallian industry supply functions and Keynes's aggregate demand curve from Marshallian micro-market demand curves even when wages and prices were flexible.[35] (A textbook explanation of Weintraub's derivation of Keynes's aggregate supply and aggregate demand curves from Marshall's microfunctions is specified in Davidson.[36])

Weintraub, following Keynes, argued that making Walrasian analysis the general theory and Keynes a special case robbed Keynes's analysis of its theoretical bite.

SUMMING UP

Finally, as one who attended the King's College, Cambridge conference celebrating the 100th anniversary of Keynes's birth, I can provide further evidence of Samuelson's arrogance at believing he had discovered the essential foundations for all economic theory. At this conference, I challenged Samuelson on his claim that Walras provided the microfoundations of Keynes's general theory. Samuelson responded with derogatory words for the analysis of what he called "unreconstructed Keynesians." Samuelson specifically named Joan Robinson and Sidney Weintraub as "unreconstructed Keynesians" whose analysis was faulty. Samuelson claimed that he and his followers are "reconstructed Keynesians" who are the only ones who correctly reconstructed Keynes's principle of effective demand on the basis of Walrasian analysis.

Paul Samuelson saved the term "Keynesian" from being excoriated by post Second World War textbooks by the McCarthy anti-communist movement at the time. But the cost of such a saving was to sever the meaning of Keynes's theory in mainstream economic theory from its *General Theory* analytical roots. These roots demonstrated that, in a money using economy, flexible wages and prices and pure competition are neither necessary nor sufficient conditions to assure full employment equilibrium, even in the long run.

Samuelson's view of Keynesianism resulted in aborting Keynes's revolutionary analysis from altering the foundation of mainstream macroeconomics as it is taught in academia. Consequently, what passes as conventional macroeconomic wisdom of mainstream economists at the beginning of the 21st century is nothing more than a high-tech and more mathematical version of 19th-century classical theory.

Sidney Weintraub's development of Post Keynesian theory was fighting against Samuelson's false and misleading macroeconomic analysis. As a student of Weintraub, I can declare that Weintraub believed that Samuelson's Walrasian version was not only wrong –

but encouraged poor policy decisions when recession and significant unemployment reared its ugly head.

Current economic policies, such as "austerity" and fears of government deficits, adopted in the United States and the Eurozone are not what Keynes's theory would recommend. Such policies have resulted in the severe and prolonged economic damage that some have called "the Great Recession." Samuelson's "reconstructed" Keynesianism, however, supposedly provided the correct analytical foundations for understanding the world we live in. Yet Samuelson's "Keynesianism" is based on Walrasian fundamentals and consequently it encourages the belief that government policies should promote government budgets that are balanced at least over the business cycle – if not every fiscal year. Instead, had Sidney Weintraub's Post Keynesian explanation of Keynes's general theory been taken up by mainstream economists and politicians, the world we live in would be controlled by significantly better monetary and fiscal policies. The result would have been that we would now be experiencing a more prosperous and civilized economic society.

In the next chapters we will develop the Keynes–Post Keynesian policies for dealing with the major economic issues that rear their ugly heads from time to time, for example, unemployment and inflation, trade policy and the balance of payments, and the growing inequality of income in Organisation for Economic Co-operation and Development (OECD) nations.

NOTES

1. H. Hoover, *The Memoirs of Herbert Hoover, The Great Depression 1929–1941* (Macmillan, New York, 1952) p. 30.
2. J. M. Keynes, *The General Theory of Employment, Interest and Money* (Macmillan, London, 1936) Chapters 19, 20.
3. P. A. Samuelson, *Foundations of Economic Analysis* (Harvard University Press, Cambridge, MA, 1947).
4. D. C. Colander and H. Landreth, *The Coming of Keynesianism to America* (Edward Elgar, Cheltenham, UK and Brookfield, VT, 1996) p. 23.
5. L. Tarshis, *The Elements of Economics* (Houghton Mifflin, New York, 1947).
6. W. F. Buckley, *God and Man at Yale* (Henry Rigney, Chicago, 1951).
7. C–L, 1996, pp. 145–178.
8. C–L, 1996, p. 172.
9. P. A. Samuelson, *Economics: An Introductory Analysis* (McGraw-Hill, New York, 1948).
10. J. M. Keynes, *The General Theory*, pp. 177, 179.

11. C–L, 1996, p. 154.
12. C–L, 1996, pp. 154–155.
13. C–L, 1996, pp. 39–48.
14. C–L, 1996, p. 43.
15. C–L, 1996, pp. 44–46.
16. C–L, 1996, p. 158.
17. C–L, 1996, p. 159.
18. C–L, 1996, pp. 159–160, emphasis added.
19. C–L, 1996, p. 160.
20. C–L, 1996, p. 161.
21. J. G. Dunlop, "The Movement of Real and Money Wages," *Economic Journal*, *58*, 1938.
22. J. M. Keynes, "Relative Movements of Real Wages and Output," *Economic Journal, 49*, 1939, reprinted in *The Collected Writings of John Maynard Keynes, 14*, edited by D. Moggridge (Macmillan, London, 1973). All references are to the reprinted version.
23. Keynes, 1973 reprint, p. 411.
24. J. M. Keynes, *The General Theory*, 1936, p. 257.
25. Keynes, 1936, p. 257.
26. Keynes, 1936, p. 259.
27. Keynes, 1936, pp. 259–260.
28. In Keynes's general theory analysis, if the money wage rate and therefore wage income declines this must reduce each worker's demand for goods and services. Even if product prices declined in line with the rate of decline in money wages, workers spending out of their reduced money income will not produce a market increase in the total quantity demanded for producible goods and services necessary for entrepreneurs to desire to increase employment.
29. C–L, 1996, p. 64.
30. Samuelson, 1947, pp. 122–124.
31. P. A. Samuelson, "Classical Economics and Neoclassical Theory," in *Monetary Theory*, edited by R. W. Clower (Penguin, London, 1969) p. 184.
32. C–L, 1996, p. 163.
33. Keynes, 1936, p. 3.
34. J. M. Keynes, *The General Theory of Employment, Interest and Money*, German edition (Duncker and Humboldt, Berlin, 1936) p. ix.
35. S. Weintraub, *An Approach to the Theory of Income Distribution* (Chilton, Philadelphia, 1958).
36. P. Davidson, *Post Keynesian Macroeconomic Theory*, 2nd edition (Edward Elgar, Cheltenham, UK and Northampton, MA, 2011).

6. Creating full employment policies

The cause of persistent unemployment in the economy is a shortage of aggregate market demand for all the products and services industry can produce at full employment. It is, therefore, obvious that government must develop policies to assure there will always be sufficient market demand to encourage entrepreneurs to believe that it will be profitable to hire all workers who want a job. This means creating additional market demand by policies that (1) produce incentives for private sector decision makers to spend more by either reducing the savings propensity of some groups in the private sector or by encouraging some decision makers to borrow to spend more, that is, by encouraging dissavings, and/or (2) provide more spending by government deficit spending on investment projects that provide useful services for the population.

Monetary policy can encourage additional borrowing. An easy monetary policy that lowers the market rate of interest on various types of loans can encourage private sector spending decisions. Unfortunately, encouraging some forms of loans to induce additional private sector spending may not always produce permanent good consequences. For example, permitting households to spend more on producible goods and services by increasing significantly their credit card debt can create problems. With the recession resulting from the financial collapse of 2007–2008, many households lost jobs and incomes and therefore faced increased difficulties in paying their credit card obligations. The result was an increase in credit card defaults and ultimately even less total spending by household borrowers.

The only private sector borrowers that government policies may encourage hoping that significant future defaults are unlikely are entrepreneurial investors. These borrowers typically obtain loans to pay for building more plant and equipment to produce more products and/or research and development of new and better products that they expect will be what people want and therefore can be profitably sold. Borrowing to finance such investment projects will take place only if self-interested managers expect to earn significantly large additional profits so that servicing such loans and repaying the principal in the future can be readily done. Unfortunately, since the future is uncertain, there is no guarantee that borrowing to finance these investment purchases will be sufficiently profitable to make servicing the debt assured. Thus, such a policy can be successful initially only if enough entre-preneurs have what Keynes called sufficient "animal spirits," that is, managers have optimistic expectations about future market demand sufficient to encourage them to take investment action purchases. In other words, these investors must see that the use of these loans will produce investment that will be easily self-liquidating.

Government can also develop fiscal policies to encourage add-itional spending by private sector decision makers. For example, a cut in the income tax rate will result in taxpaying households having additional after-tax income that they can then spend on additional purchases of goods and services.

Classical oriented economic theorists, however, have developed a theory called the "Ricardian equivalence thesis" to argue that cutting personal income taxes will not encourage any additional household spending. Under the Ricardian equivalence thesis, it is argued that since households have correct expectations about the future, they will know that the government will have to increase taxes in the future in order to pay for the deficit caused today by cutting taxes without reducing government spending. Accordingly, these hypothetical "rational" household taxpayers will save their increases in after-tax income after a tax cut in order to have sufficient funds to pay the higher future tax rates they expect government to require to pay off the current deficit.

Therefore, no additional spending will be stimulated by an immediate reduction in personal income taxes for classical econo-mists who believe in this Ricardian equivalence theory. Instead, the only significant effect of a tax cut will be an increase in the total government deficit and debt since the government receives less in tax revenue due to the individual tax cut but continues to spend at the same rate as before.

Keynes and the Post Keynesians, on the other hand, would argue that a tax cut will provide some stimulus since for every additional dollar in after-tax income, some fraction of the tax cut will be spent and a small portion will be saved. For example, if a taxpayer received a tax reduction of say $100, then his/her after-tax take home income rises by $100. It is assumed that some amount of this additional after-tax income, say $90, will be spent to buy more goods and services – thereby stimulating the creation of $90 of additional income for firms and workers. The household will save the other $10 in the form of liquid assets.

On the other hand, if instead of giving a tax cut of $100 the government spent that $100 on buying additional goods and services produced by domestic firms and workers, then this would stimulate the immediate creation of an additional $100 of income for firms and workers. Accordingly, every dollar of deficit created by increasing government spending by a dollar will always produce a greater stimulus for employment than a similar sized deficit created by providing a tax cut.

MAKING DOLLARS AND SENSE OF THE US GOVERNMENT DEBT

The moral of the Keynes–Post Keynesian theory is, as we have noted, that full employment requires business firms to be expecting sufficient market demand for their goods and services so that they can sell all they can produce at a profit. Whenever some decision makers decide to save more, that is, not spending all their income on the products of industry, then, if there is to be no increase in unemployment, there must be other decision makers who dissave by the same amount as the extra savings done by the savers, that is, dissavers must spend ever more than their current income, in order to maintain profitable market demand.

If, by borrowing, business firms engage in sufficient investment spending, then full employment can be maintained while this dissaving by business firms should be ultimately funded by the sale of debt or equity financial securities to savers directly or indirectly via financial institutions that invest in the financial assets for these savers (e.g., pension funds, mutual funds, banks). If the magnitude of this financed investment spending in the economy is less than what people want to save out of the income they would earn at full employment income, then the market demand for goods and services will not be sufficient to maintain full employment. If, however, there is still another spender(s) who spends more than current income (i.e., dissaves) sufficiently to make total dissaving in the system equal to total planned savings at the full employment level, then full employment prosperity is assured. In other words, there must be found sufficient sources of (dissaving) spending on goods and services to offset the aggregate propensity to save of the nation if the economy is not to decline into recession and possible depression.

The dissaving spender of last resort should be the federal government for it has the responsibility to take action to make sure that the nation's business firms will want to hire all who are willing to work. Moreover, as long as the nation uses it own currency to settle contractual obligations, then the federal government can always pay all its debt serving contractual agreements if necessary by borrowing funds from the central bank – which after all is an agency created by the federal government.

First, the government should engage in policies that are directed to encourage business firms to expect a rapidly growing market demand for their products so that they want to spend more on investment in plant and equipment to produce things that the market wants. If, for whatever reason, business firms will not invest sufficiently to produce full employment, then it is the responsibility of the government to deficit spend in order to create additional market demand for the products of industry. Hopefully, this additional (dissaving) spending by government will be on useful projects, for example, building and maintaining infrastructure such as bridges, roads, sewer systems, parks and public education.

When government deficit spends, that is, spends more than tax receipts, then the total size of the national debt will increase while the savings of the domestic population generally rises as the population receives more income from which they can save some portion. Some politicians claim that a rising public debt will ultimately bankrupt the nation.

No economic topic has encouraged more political demagoguery than the claim that the nation's deficits contribute to an "unsustainable" growth in the total national debt of the federal government which can ultimately lead to bankruptcy. Those who proclaim the unsustainability of a growing national debt argue that any presidential administration must be very cautious in recommending any additional spending stimulus programs to reduce significantly the rate of unemployment to avoid recession or depression. The proponents of this debt issue unsustainability argument use the analogy of comparing the federal government to a private household where the latter will always find that it will be unsustainable to let its total debt grow faster than its income.

We all should remember the advice Mr. Micawber gave about household happiness and spending when he told David Copperfield, "Annual income twenty pounds, annual expenditure nineteen six, result happiness. Annual income twenty pounds, annual expenditure twenty pounds ought and six, result misery." Mr. Micawber was specifying that a household should never spend more than its income. As Keynes explained, however, what is true for a household is not necessarily true for a nation. A sage once said: "Those who cannot remember the past are condemned to repeat its errors." So let us review the past history of the national debt of the United States to make sure we avoid its errors and repeat its successes.

Is the National Debt too Large and Unsustainable?

In 1790 the newly founded US government assumed the debts that had been incurred during the Revolutionary War. Thus, from the very beginning of the United States as a nation, the federal government accepted a national debt obligation that was approximately $75 million – a very large sum in those days. In 1835, the seventh president of the United States, President Jackson submitted a budget for the fiscal year 1835 to Congress that when enacted reduced the national debt to close to a zero balance. By 1837, the economy went into a steep recession that lasted approximately six years, and the national debt increased dramatically as tax revenues declined more rapidly than government spending. Since then the US government has always had a significant outstanding national debt owed to its citizens.

During the First World War the national debt increased substantially from approximately $4 billion in 1916 to over $27 billion by 1919. The prosperous full employment decade of the 1920s, often called the "roaring twenties," saw a tremendous increase in private sector spending on goods and services. The result was a large reduction in the national debt as annual tax receipts exceeded government spending. By 1929 the total debt had been reduced by 37 percent from over $27 billion to $16.9 billion. This 1920s' experience indicates that when the private sector is spending sufficiently to buy all the products that industry can produce in a fully employed economy, then there is no need for the government to deficit spend merely to maintain a prosperous economy. The government may actually be able to run a surplus and start paying down the national debt as it did during the roaring twenties.

The 1920s' prosperity and consequent large tax revenues, however, were partly the result of significant bubbles in the stock market and in private sector real estate finance and development. (Shades of the prosperous US economy of the 1990s and early 2000s, where the dot.com security bubble of the 1990s and the housing bubble of early 2000s encouraged a rapid growth in private sector spending.)

When in 1929 private sector spending on produced goods and services suddenly slowed, the result was a devastating drop in business profits. Unemployment rose rapidly as the United States entered the Great Depression. Tax revenues fell from $4 billion in 1930 to less than $2 billion in 1932. When President Roosevelt took office in 1933, the national debt was almost $20 billion; a sum equal to 33 percent of US GDP at the time.

During its first term in office, the Roosevelt Administration ran large annual deficits of between 2 and 5 percent of GDP. By 1936 the national debt had increased to $33.7 billion, or approximately 40 percent of GDP, even as the unemployment rate was significantly reduced. Many "experts" of that era said the growth of the national debt was unsustainable. Disaster awaited the nation if the government continued to deficit spend and thereby burden future generations with this huge debt. Accordingly, as a part of his 1936 reelection campaign, Roosevelt's fiscal year 1937 budget submitted to Congress in 1936 cut government spending dramatically. As a result, in 1937 the economy fell into a steep recession. Tax revenues declined and the national debt increased to $37 billion. The government resumed significant planned deficit spending in 1938 and the economy started to recover. By 1940, the economy had grown substantially while the national debt rose to $43 billion – approximately 44 percent of GDP.

When the United States entered the Second World War in 1941, the fear of deficits and the size of the national debt were forgotten. The most important thing was to defeat the enemy. In the war years, from 1941 to 1945, GDP doubled while the national debt increased by more than 500 percent as Roosevelt financed much of the war expenditures by government borrowing. By the end of the war in 1945, the national debt had increased to $258 billion and was approximately 116 percent of GDP.

Rather than bankrupting the nation, this large growth in the national debt promoted a prosperous economy. By 1946 the average American household was living much better economically than in the pre-war days. Moreover, the children of that Depression– Second World War generation were not burdened by having to pay off what then was considered a huge national debt. Instead, for the next quarter of a century, the economy continued on a path of unprecedented economic growth and prosperity, with the Eisenhower Administration launching the biggest peacetime public works project – the interstate highway system.

The Kennedy–Johnson Administration spent large sums on sending a man to the moon and the escalating Vietnam War. At the same time, the inequality in the distribution of income was significantly reduced. For more than two decades after the war, the United States experienced a golden age of economic development as the rich grew richer while the poor gained even more with a rapidly rising level of income that created a large American middle class.

As a child of the depression and a young teenager during the Second World War, I have never felt burdened by the huge government deficits that accrued due to government spending during the Great Depression and the war that followed. The legacy that the Great Generation that included my parents (those who were adults during the depression and the war) left to their children like me was an economy of abundance and prosperity. I inherited an economy that made finding a good job easy for me and all of my cohorts, and it provided excellent opportunities to improve our living standards. If this is burdening children and grandchildren, I hope the current generation can create such a "burden" for their progeny.

The moral of this history of the national debt and the economy during the Great Depression and the Second World War is that we have nothing to fear about running big government deficits when, during a recession with significant unemployment, the federal government is the only spender that can take the responsibility to deficit spend to sufficiently increase the market demand for the products of our industries and thereby maintain a profitable entrepreneurial system. If the government was to spend less in the hopes of keeping down the size of the national debt, then the result will cause market demand to remain slack, thereby impoverishing both our business firms and our workers. The basic message of Keynes's theory is that capitalism works best when spenders cause healthy growth in market demands and thereby generate profits and jobs for the community.

This was clearly demonstrated when government spending increased during the years 1933–1936 and 1938–1945. When Roosevelt cut spending in 1937, the sharp 1937 recession showed that, at that stage of recovery, no other spenders were willing or able to take over from government the role of spending more than they were earning and thereby generate additional market demand and profits for American businesses. Had Roosevelt, in 1938, continued on the path of keeping government spending in check in order not to increase the total national debt, the result would have been to propagate the poorly performing economy of 1937. When the Second World War broke out, and no further thought was given to the size of the national debt, government spending quickly pushed the economy to a continuous profitable full employment status. Keynes's ideas that the role of government fiscal policy was to make sure that the total market demand for goods and services provided profit opportunities to encourage business firms to hire all workers who wanted a job was validated by this historical record.

Business firms will hire more workers only when they expect or know that the market demand for their products is increasing. Today, who are these buyers who will be willing to buy significantly more products from factories located in the United States in order to completely end the current Great Recession by restoring full employment prosperity? Clearly, households suffering from high unemployment, decreasing market values for their homes, large credit card debt and shrinking pension funds are not likely to rush to buy a large amount of additional goods and services. Entrepreneurs with existing excess facilities, even if after several years of depressed demand they are still experiencing, at best, not rapidly rising market demands, are unlikely to invest significantly more in new plant and equipment. Moreover, foreign countries, such as China with its large savings of US dollar earnings, appear unlikely to spend more dollars to buy more US produced export goods. With falling property and sales taxes revenues, local and state governments are more likely to cut spending on public services and reduce purchases from domestically located firms. Only the federal government can afford to buy significant additional products to stimulate market demand for domestically produced goods and services.

Just as citizens should expect the federal government to spend whatever is necessary to protect them from foreign enemies during a war, or even terrorist attacks in peacetime, they should also expect the government to spend whatever is necessary to protect them from the economic terrorism of a recession or depression. The public must be educated to understand that a civilized society is one that assures that both domestic enterprises and workers will prosper, and that the intelligent use of government fiscal policy can assure that total market demand is always sufficient to generate domestic profits large enough to create a fully employed economy.

Some argue that tax revenues must finance all government spending so that the federal budget is always balanced without deficits, or at least that annual deficits do not increase the debt to GDP ratio. As history shows, however, even during the Second World War when America was attacked by foreign nations (remember Pearl Harbor?), the US government did not finance the entire defense of this nation by raising taxes. Instead, during the war years, deficits expanded dramatically while no one worried (correctly) about burdening future generations with debt.

If wars are not sufficient (or necessary) reasons to raise taxes or cut government spending sufficiently to balance the budget while protecting the nation, then why should defending the nation against serious economic threats require a balanced budget or perhaps a lower deficit? Our politicians and the public must be educated to understand that when total private sector spending creates a market demand for domestically produced goods that is so small as to threaten recession and depression, then government must deficit spend as much as necessary to encourage domestic entrepreneurs to hire all American workers who are willing and able to work. If, on the other hand, market demand for domestically produced goods and services were to exceed America's full employment productive capacity, then government must increase taxes and reduce spending in order to reduce aggregate demand to a level that can be met by a fully employed labor force.

When the public and politicians recognize that a primary function of government fiscal policy is to act as a balancing wheel to assure that aggregate market demand will be sufficient to encourage America's entrepreneurs to create jobs for all our workers, we will have developed the political will to develop a perpetually prosperous American civilized society. At that point of time, our next task will be to develop an international financial and payments system that will provide for global full employment and prosperity.

7. Inflation policy

Keynes's general theory analysis was developed in the 1930s after Britain had suffered more than a decade of high unemployment and depression – and not inflation. It is not surprising therefore that Keynes devoted most of the theoretical analysis in his general theory to curing the unemployment problem and relegated his discussion of changes in the price level to Chapter 21 entitled "The Theory of Prices." In this chapter of his book, as a student of Alfred Marshall, Keynes suggests that rising prices of newly produced goods and services are primarily due to the same forces Marshall believed explained why the price of the products of a firm would increase. These inflationary aspects occurred when, at any point of time, enterprise expanded its production and this resulted in (1) "diminishing returns" or "bottlenecks" in production and therefore increasing production costs and/or (2) increases in the money "wage unit," that is, a money wage rate increase that caused higher labor production costs per unit of output.

Since Keynes had explicitly rejected the classical neutral money axiom in 1933,[1] his theory of inflation cannot be the classical theory where it is changes in the quantity of money relative to the level of output that directly affects the price level. Inflation in classical theory is solely the result of "too much money chasing too few goods." The classical cure for inflation is for the nation's central bank to cut back the supply of money so that there are fewer dollars to chase the available goods. If the economy suffers from deflation, that is, falling prices, then the classical theory explanation is that there is too little money chasing too many goods. The implication is therefore that to end deflation, or to achieve a target rate of inflation rate that the central bank believes desirable, monetary policy should increase the quantity of money.

In this chapter we will explain why the neutral money theory analysis of inflation or deflation is not applicable to the economy in which we live. We will leave until Chapter 9 the analysis of how international trade also can affect the price level of the goods that domestic households purchase for consumption purposes.

In Keynes's analysis, money is never neutral in either the short run or the long run. Consequently, Keynes's general theory suggests that unless the economy is already at full employment, any monetary policy that increases the quantity of money in the system can impact directly on real economic production and employment outcomes rather than on the price level. In Keynes's theory, only when the economy is already at full employment and production of goods and services cannot be increased will an increase in the money supply lead to the possibility of inflation.

In 2014, central bankers in the United States and the Eurozone indicated that the problem was either actual price deflation or, at least, the economy was below their targeted desired rate of inflation. Only if these central bankers accept the neutral money axiom can they believe that only by increasing the quantity of money per se will the system achieve what they perceive is the proper target rate of inflation.

On the other hand, the Keynes–Post Keynesian theory states that whenever there is persistent unemployment in the system the proper target of central bank monetary policy is (1) to create and maintain sufficient liquidity in the system and (2) to encourage dissaving (borrowing) by private sector decision makers in the hopes they will spend the borrowed funds on the products of industry. This will increase market demand and induce enterprises to hire more workers.

As early as 1930, Keynes wrote that bank "credit is the pavement along which production travels, and the bankers if they knew their duty, would provide the transport facilities to just the extent that is required in order that the productive powers of the community can be employed at their full capacity."[2] As long as the economy is at less than full employment, the central bank should think of increases in the quantity of money supply as a stimulus to investment spending and increasing employment. Until the economy obtains and can maintain full employment, the primary function of any central bank, as controller of the banking system, is to encourage bankers to make credit (liquidity) available as cheaply as possible to those who want to borrow in order to buy more goods and services in the market place. As long as the economy has significant idle resources that could be gainfully employed, monetary policy should facilitate spending to encourage economic expansion and growth. The central bank's function is not to set a target for the observed rate of price level inflation before full employment is achieved.

The only way the central bank can attempt to reduce the observed inflation rate is if it increases interest rates and restricts bank credit sufficiently to substantially reduce aggregate market demand spending on the products of business firms. As employers produce less in response to lower market demand, there may be some reduction of the rate of inflation simply by indirectly eliminating bottlenecks and reducing diminishing returns. But the primary effect of tightening the monetary policy to reduce the rate of inflation is to create enough slack in labor markets to encourage employers to resist any labor demands for an increase in the money wage rates that would result in increasing unit production costs and product prices. With enough slack in the labor markets to produce widespread unemployment, workers who are still employed are not likely to risk losing their jobs by demanding higher wages when they know there are many unemployed who would gladly take their jobs at their current money wage rate.

Let us develop this often neglected aspect of Keynes's theory.

CONTRACTS, PRICES AND INFLATION

Our earlier discussion of the importance of money and the use of spot and forward contracts provides us with the platform for explaining the cause(s) of inflation in the real world. In all modern money using economies, all market production and exchange transactions are organized via money contracts in either a spot market or a forward (or futures) market. Accordingly, at any point of calendar time, there may exist simultaneously two sets of prices for producible goods. These are (1) the spot price[3] for immediate delivery and payment of the product and (2) the forward price[4] that is today's contractual agreed on prices to pay at a specific future date (or dates) when payment and product delivery is contractually agreed upon. Since production takes some period of calendar time before the final goods can appear in the market, spot prices will deal with commodities already produced and being held in inventory for immediate sale on the market. Forward prices will be associated with goods whose production will begin if the buyer is willing to enter a contractual order to receive delivery when the product is finished and comes off the end of the production line.

Alfred Marshall, the teacher of Keynes, noted that spot market prices could be at any level that cleared the market for instant delivery, that is, the spot price where every unit of output is willingly held by some person or business firm – even if the spot price does not cover the costs of production experienced in producing this inventory. On the other hand, the forward or short-run price is the offer price of sellers that buyers must be willing to accept in order to place the forward contractual order. With that contractual order in hand, the seller will undertake the necessary productive activity to assure the product will be available for delivery at the specific contractual future date. In other words, all forward prices are associated with the necessary money costs of production (including profits) that are required to be paid to the business firm to encourage entrepreneurs to hire enough productive inputs to achieve a specific production output target at a specific point of time. It should be noted that in the world of experience it is a stylized fact that, except at the retail level, almost all production is related to forward contractual orders received by the producer/ seller.

In his earlier *Treatise on Money*,[5] Keynes had identified two types of inflation and/or deflation: *commodity inflation (or deflation)* and *incomes inflation (or deflation)*. Commodity inflation was identified with rising spot market prices over time where at any immediate point of time only pre-existing stocks of goods can be sold on the market. Since production takes some duration of calendar time to occur, if there is a sudden increase in spot market demand for products, there can be no available augmentation of existing stocks for immediate delivery to constrain this spot market inflation. The immediate result is commodity spot price inflation. (If commodity inflation has occurred, then holders of the pre-existing durable producibles can sell their inventory at a higher spot price than previously and thereby obtain a capital gain on their holdings.)

The second form of inflation, *incomes inflation*, is associated with rising prices that are associated with increases in the money costs of production and/or profit margin associated with each unit of goods produced. These money costs of production represent the income payments to wage and salary earners, material suppliers, lenders and profit recipients. In other words, if the money costs per unit of production increase and are being paid, then owners of the inputs to the production process are receiving higher money incomes.

One of the most widely used forward contracts is the labor hiring contract where entrepreneurs agree to pay workers a specified money wage per unit of labor per hour, or per week or even per annum, for the duration of the labor contract.

This incomes inflation taxonomy highlights the obvious but oft neglected fact that, given productivity relations, inflationary increases in the prices of domestic producible goods are always associated with (and the result of) an increase in some domestic resident's money income earned in the production process. Often this incomes inflation is associated with increases in the money wages paid to workers via a forward labor hiring contract. If this wage increase is greater than any productivity increase per worker then the costs of production must have risen. Accordingly, if the nation is to adopt a policy of achieving a specific targeted rate of inflation of domestically producible goods, one must somehow have a policy – an incomes policy – which constrains the rise in the money income of owners of inputs including wage rates in domestic production processes.

THE INFLATION PROCESS IN A KEYNES WORLD

Spot prices, by definition, move in step with immediate changes in the market demand for immediate delivery of existing products. Thus, at any moment in calendar time, every unexpected sudden increase in demand for products and/or services for immediate delivery should produce an increase in spot prices, while a fall in market demand for immediate delivery will result in a commodity price deflation.

It is, however, the effect on forward – not spot – prices that is most important for explaining a continuing (over calendar time) inflation problem with the prices of goods and services that most households buy. No matter how high spot prices go at any point of calendar time, if forward prices remain stable, then if buyers are willing to wait the gestation period for the production of additional output, buyers can always order today newly produced goods and services for delivery at a future date at today's forward (supply) price offered by enterprises. If, despite any hypothetical increase in spot demand, the costs of production, and therefore the forward prices, remain stable over time, then the spot price inflation can only be a temporary (market period) phenomenon that will be diminished when additional finished product is available for sale in the spot market place. Moreover, to the extent that the spot price of commodities with long gestation periods are the inflation problem, and there is no spillover causing a rise in the money costs of production, then the policy solution for inflation is the holding by the government of buffer stocks.

Since a spot or commodity price inflation occurs whenever there is a sudden and unforeseen change in demand or available supply *for immediate delivery*, this type of inflation can easily be avoided if there is some institution that is not motivated by self-interest but instead maintains a "buffer stock" to prevent unforeseen changes in spot demand and supply from inducing significant spot price movements. A buffer stock is nothing more than some commodity shelf-inventory that can be moved into and out of the spot market to buffer the market from disorderly price disruptions by offsetting the unforeseen changes in spot demand or supply.

For example, since the oil price shocks of the 1970s, the US government has developed a "strategic petroleum reserve." The government bought crude oil in the market and stored these crude oil inventories in underground salt domes on the coast of the Gulf of Mexico. These strategic petroleum reserves were designed to be held in inventories to provide emergency market oil supplies to buffer the domestic oil spot market if there is a sudden decrease in oil supplies from the politically unstable Middle East that threatens to encourage additional speculative demand for oil on the spot oil commodity market. The strategic use of such a petroleum reserve means that the spot price of oil will not increase as much as it otherwise would if, for example, a political crisis broke out in the Middle East. Spot oil price inflation could be avoided as long as the buffer stock exists to offset any potentially threatening, immediately available commodity shortage. During the short Desert Storm war against Iraq in 1991, United States government officials made strategic petroleum reserves available to the commodity oil market to offset the possibility of disruptions (actual or expected) from affecting the spot price of crude oil. The Department of Energy estimated that this use of the strategic petroleum reserve as a buffer stock in 1991, during the brief Desert Storm period, prevented the price of gasoline at the pump from rising about 30 cents per gallon.

Use of buffer stocks as a public policy solution to spot price inflation or deflation is as old as the biblical story of Joseph and the Pharaoh's dream of seven fat cows followed by seven lean cows. Joseph – the economic forecaster of his day – interpreted the Pharaoh's dream as portending seven good harvests, where production would be much above normal and market prices (and therefore farmers' incomes) below normal, followed by seven lean harvests, where annual production would not provide enough food to go around while prices farmers received would be exorbitantly high. Joseph's civilized policy proposal for avoiding inflation and deflation in food prices was for the government to build up and store a *buffer stock* of grain during the good years and release the grain to market, without profit, during the bad years. This would maintain a stable price over the 14 harvests and avoid inflation in the bad years while protecting farmer's incomes in the good harvest years. The Bible records that this civilized buffer stock policy to stabilize commodity prices and farmers' income over a period of 14 years was a resounding economic success.

INCOMES INFLATION

Increases in money wages, salaries and other material costs in production contracts always imply an increase in someone's money income. The costs of production of a firm are the other side of the coin of the income of people who provide labor or other resources for use by the firm in the production process. A cost of production is always someone's income!

With slavery illegal in civilized societies, the money wage contract for hiring labor is the most universal of all production costs. Labor cost accounts for the vast majority of production contract costs in the economy, even for such high-tech products as NASA spacecraft. That is why, especially during the first four decades after the Second World War, consumer price inflation was usually associated with money wage inflation.

Wage contracts specify a certain money wage per unit of time over the duration of the contract. This labor cost plus a profit margin or mark-up to cover material costs, overheads and profit on the investment become the basis for managerial decisions as to the prices they must receive on a forward sales contract to make the undertaking worthwhile in terms of covering costs and returning a profit. If money wages rise relative to the productivity of labor, then the labor costs of producing each unit of outputs increase. Consequently, firms must raise their sales (forward) contract price if they are to maintain profitability and viability. When any production costs per unit of output are increasing, then forward contract prices for orders for produced goods and services are rising throughout the economy. The economy is suffering a forward contract or *incomes inflation*.

To prevent incomes inflation there must be some constraint on the rate of increase of money incomes relative to productivity. This requires some form of incomes policy.

INCOMES POLICY

For several decades after the Second World War, money wage rates were increasing faster than labor productivity in most developed nations. This was a major factor in the incomes inflation these nations experienced. To understand why this was so prevalent at that time, we must recognize the change in the nature of the industrial society that came after the Second World War. As John Kenneth Galbraith noted, "The market with its maturing of industrial society and its associated political institutions ... loses radically its authority as a regulatory force ... [and] partly it is an expression of our democratic ethos."[6]

After the devastating loss of income experience most households endured during the Great Depression of the 1930s, the emerging ethos of the common man in democratic nations held that people should have more control of their economic destiny. The Great Depression had taught that individuals cannot have control of their economic lives if they leave the determination of their income completely to the tyranny of the free market. Consequently, after the Second World War, in societies with any democratic tendencies, people not only demanded economic security from their economic system but they also demanded to play a controlling role in determining their economic life. This required power to control one's income. The result was an institutional power struggle for higher money incomes between unions, political coalitions, economic cartels and monopolistic industries. When these power struggles lead to demands for higher incomes at any level of production, the result is incomes inflation.

As long as the government guarantees that it will pursue a full employment policy, then each self-interested worker, union and business entrepreneur has less to fear that their demand for higher prices and money income will result in significantly fewer sales, less income and more unemployment. As long as the government accepts the responsibility for creating sufficient aggregate effective demand to maintain the economy close to a full employment level of output, there may be no market incentive to stop this recurring struggle over the distribution of income.

Full employment policies without some deliberately announced incomes constraint policy assures that there would no longer exist what Marx called "the industrial reserve army" of the unemployed to constrain the demands of employed workers for higher wages. In a *laissez-faire* market environment, employers are free to choose to hire workers from the pool of unemployed to replace workers currently employed. In this free market system, a significantly large industrial reserve army of the unemployed can be a major force that constrains organized workers' demand for higher money wages.

In an open economy where free trade exists and multinational enterprises make important decisions regarding where geographically production is to take place, foreign workers who earn wages significantly below that of domestic workers can act as the equivalent of a Marxian "industrial reserve army" to keep domestic money wages depressed and many domestic workers unemployed. Since the 1990s, with a continuous push for globalized free trade, the almost unlimited supply of unskilled and semi-skilled workers in countries such as China and India willing to work for much lower wages than those that prevail in the West have acted similar to a Marxist "industrialized army of the unemployed" in limiting Western workers' ability to even maintain, on average, the existing money wage rate. (We will discuss possible policy solutions for this problem of outsourcing production to emerging economies with low paid workers in Chapter 10.) Consequently, by the beginning of the

21st century, the threat of runaway high rates of incomes inflation due to inflationary money wage increases had fallen off the radar screen of most OECD nations. In fact, price deflation has become an increasingly important depressing factor in Western developed nations.

For those classical economists who believe in the beneficence of the "invisible hand" of free markets, there is only one way to combat any incomes inflation that may occur in our economy. In a free society where people are motivated solely by self-interest, workers and entrepreneurs are free to organize to demand a higher price for their services, even if such demands are inflationary. As the former prime minister of the United Kingdom, Mrs. Thatcher, was often quoted as saying, "One of the rights of a free society is the right to price oneself out of the market."

In the decades immediately after the Second World War, restraining inflationary wage demands by workers, often via their unions, and entrepreneurs lacking significant competition in the market place, required a policy where the nation's central bank constrained the banking system from providing all the working capital finance necessary to pay these inflationary income demands. The resulting lack of sufficient effective market demand did create a situation where those demanding higher money incomes were, as Mrs. Thatcher had stated, often priced out of the market.

If an independent central bank adamantly refuses to increase the money supply sufficiently to finance inflationary income demands of owners of domestic factors of production, then the resultant slack demand in the market place for domestic goods and services will discipline all workers and firms with the fear of loss of sales and income. The hope is that this fear will keep wage and price increases in check. To make this fear credible, central banks have adopted a policy of telling the public that they have a target of some inflation rate. If the observed inflation rate exceeds the central bank's target, then the central bank implies that it will institute a restrictive monetary policy sufficient to reduce market demand so that domestic firms feel threatened with less profitable market conditions and workers with unemployment. Nothing closely approaching full employment prosperity can be tolerated as long as we rely on the central bank's free market incomes policy of threatening workers with unemployment and enterprise with falling profit levels. Thus, those who advocate that central banks publically announce a low "inflation target" on which the monetary policy will depend are implicitly endorsing an incomes policy based on creating fear expectations of loss of jobs, sales revenues and profits for firms that produce goods and services domestically. Fear, it is believed, will keep owners of the domestic factors of production in their place. The amount of slack demand necessary to enforce this *incomes policy of fear* will depend on what some modern classical economists call the domestic *natural rate of unemployment*.

Accordingly, proponents of this inflation targeting incomes policy of fear are implicitly suggesting that the natural unemployment rate will be smaller if government "liberalizes" labor markets by reducing, if not completely eliminating, long-term unemployment benefits or other money income supports including minimum wages, employer contributions to pension funds, health insurance for their employees, legislation protecting working conditions and so on. The belief is that workers will be less truculent and more willing to accept the existing wage structure when the government removes unemployment benefits and other income support policies.

To those who advocate such an incomes policy of fear, a permanent large social safety net is seen as mollycoddling casualties in the war against inflation so that others may think there is little to fear if they join the ranks of the unemployed. A ubiquitous and overwhelming fear instilled in all members of society is a necessary condition for the barbarous inflation targeting program to work in a period of undesirably high rates of inflation. The result is inevitably that the civil society is the first casualty.

With the integration of populous nations such as China, India and so on into the global economy of the 21st century, as we have already suggested, another "industrial reserve army" has been introduced into the economies of many OECD nations. Since the 1990s, with the almost unlimited supply of idle and unemployed workers (often including children) in these populous nations who are eager to accept jobs at wages much below those prevailing in the major OECD nations and the growing phenomena of outsourcing of manufacturing jobs and services incomes, the labor forces of major industrial nations have been significantly constrained in their wage income demands. As a result, incomes inflation has been limited to those domestic service occupations and industries and manufacturing industries (e.g., national defense) where outsourcing is not a possible alternative and the unemployment rate in the industry is relatively low.

As cheap foreign workers have often replaced higher paid domestic labor in many production processes, enterprise profit margins have been increasing. The result has been significant increases in the profit share of income, often leading to large increases in the income of senior managers and owners of many firms. The result has been a growing inequality of income between the unskilled, semi-skilled and even some skilled workers in Western industrial nations and the domestic managers and owners of multinational corporations who can engage in outsourcing of their lower end jobs and demand higher profit margins on the segment of their integrated chain that provides goods and services domestically.

What civilized anti-inflation incomes policy can one develop from Keynes's revolutionary analytic approach? In 1970, Sidney Weintraub, basing his analysis on Keynes's analytical framework[7] developed a "clever" anti-inflation policy which he called TIP, or a tax-based incomes policy.[8] TIP required the use of the corporate income tax structure to penalize the largest domestic firms in the economy if they agreed to wage rate increases in excess of some national productivity improvement standard and/or if the firms raised prices to increase profit margins significantly. Thus, the tax system would be used to penalize those firms that agreed to inflationary wage demands or profit mark-ups. The hope for TIP was that if wage increases could be limited to overall productivity increases, then workers and owners of all other inputs to the domestic production process would willingly accept non-inflationary monetary income increases. Increases in the real incomes of the owners of the factors of production would then be associated with increases in productivity.

There were two conditions that Weintraub believed were necessary if TIP was to be an effective policy that did not rely on "fear" of loss of income to constrain incomes inflation. These conditions were:

1.   TIP was to be a permanent policy institution.
2.   TIP must be a penalty system, not a reward (subsidy) tax system.

First, once instituted, TIP could never be removed, for otherwise it would become an impotent policy as it reached its termination date.

Weintraub indicated that the magnitude of the tax penalties could be altered as conditions warranted, but there must always be the existence of a threat of penalties to ensure compliance.

Second, a reward TIP, that is, one which reduced people's taxes if they adhered to the national wage standard, would be administratively unworkable, as everyone would claim the reward and it would be up to the government to prove which claimants were not entitled to the reduction in taxes. Weintraub suggested that TIP was similar to the way government enforces speed limits on the nation's highways. If one exceeds the speed limit – which is always in place – one pays a speeding fine. Governments never pay good drivers for not exceeding the speed limit.

Unfortunately, the United States and many other nations have never seriously attempted to develop a permanent penalty oriented TIP. Instead, in the last decades of the 20th century, inflation was typically fought via the typical Monetarist "incomes policy of fear," that is, restricting the growth of the money supply so as to create slack labor markets via recession. Those who raise their wages above productivity growth will then find themselves priced out of the market place.

The real cost of such a Monetarist incomes policy to many industrialized nations in the last decades of the 20th century was significant. For countries such as Germany and France, double digit unemployment rates – previously unseen since the Great Depression – became the norm.

Only in recent decades has the problem of inflationary wage demand been almost eliminated by enterprises "outsourcing" jobs to production plants in foreign nations. This outsourcing by management forces the remaining employed domestic workers to accept stagnant wage rates while being sufficiently thankful that their jobs have not been outsourced.

Weintraub, the perpetual believer in the use of human intelligence rather than brute (market) forces to encourage socially compatible civilized behavior, believed that ultimately some form of civilized incomes constraint policy would be seen as a more humane policy to control inflation without the necessary depressing side effects of traditional Monetarist policy.

In Chapter 9 on international trade, a policy will be suggested that permits a nation's labor force to be protected from the "industrial army of the unemployed" in cheap foreign labor nations and thereby provide the hope of maintaining full employment of the domestic labor force. At that time, the nation may simultaneously have to introduce a civilized incomes policy such as TIP to constrain inflationary income demands of domestic owners of the inputs into the domestic production processes as the threat of foreign cheap labor competition is reduced.

Words and concepts are important weapons in the fight against inflation. One of the most important functions of government in any anti-inflationary struggle is to educate the public of the major industrialized nations that the income distribution struggle is (in the aggregate) an uncivilized no-win game. Although there may be some relative winners for periods of time, the basic civil instincts of the nation's society will be the ultimate loser. In the absence of a sensible policy about the distribution of income nationally and internationally, the result is not a zero-sum game, but a real loss in total aggregate income nationally and internationally as governments compete via pursuing restrictive monetary and/or "austerity" fiscal policies to reduce both outstanding debt obligations domestically and, as we will discuss in Chapter 9, international debts among nations.

NOTES

1. J. M. Keynes, "A Monetary Theory of Production," 1933 reprinted in *The Collected Writings of John Maynard Keynes, 13*, edited by D. Moggridge (Macmillan, London, 1973).
2. J. M. Keynes, *A Treatise on Money, 2* (Macmillan, London, 1930) p. 220.
3. Spot prices are equivalent to what the economist Alfred Marshall labeled market period prices.
4. Forward prices are Marshall's short-run flow-supply prices.
5. J. M. Keynes, *A Treatise on Money, 1* (Macmillan, London, 1930) reprinted in *The Collected Writings of John Maynard Keynes, 5*, edited by D. Moggridge (Macmillan, London, 1971) p. 140.
6. J. K. Galbraith, "On Post Keynesian Economics," *Journal of Post Keynesian Economics, 1*, 1978, pp. 8–9.
7. S. Weintraub, *An Approach to the Theory of Income Distribution* (Chilton, Philadephia, 1958).
8. S. Weintraub, "An Incomes Policy to Stop Inflation," *Lloyds Bank Review*, 1971.

8. Securitization, liquidity and market failure

The winter of 2007–2008 proved to be a winter of discontent in global financial markets. Initially, the US subprime mortgage problem created an insolvency problem for major underwriters. The exotic financial instruments that they created, such as mortgage backed derivatives, lost liquidity and market value. This problem proved contagious as it spilled over to other exotic financial markets such as the auction rate securities markets[1] and the credit default swap markets.[2] The auction rate markets, which had seen few failures in years, suddenly experienced over a thousand failures in the early months of 2008. What caused this contagion to spill over and what was the cause for this tremendous increase in market failures?

The answer to both questions is simple. Economists and market participants had forgotten Keynes's liquidity preference theory (hereafter LPT) and had, instead, swallowed hook, line and sinker the belief that the classical efficient market theory (hereafter EMT) is the useful model for understanding the operation of real world financial markets.

The EMT suggests that all one has to do is bring informed buyers and sellers together in an unregulated, free financial market and the market price will always adjust in an orderly manner to the market clearing price, where the latter is based on readily available existing information called market "fundamentals," such as price/earnings ratios, risks of defaults and so on. This information is readily available to all via modern computer reporting of market trends and history of market behavior in the past.

Bringing the buyers and sellers together, however, requires providing a place for a well-organized and orderly market where trading between buyers and sellers can readily take place.

In the pre-computer age, financial markets required buyers and sellers to be represented by dealers who would meet in a physical location (e.g., the stock exchange) to trade. Members of these financial asset market exchanges recognized that, at any given moment of the trading day, there may be a problem of getting a sufficient number of bone fide buyers and sellers together to maintain a well-organized and orderly market. It was, therefore, necessary to adopt financial market rules that required all market participants to deal only with authorized broker-dealers that were permitted to execute trades in the specific market place. The broker-dealers acted as fiduciary agents for specific buyers or sellers to place orders with other members of the stock exchange, sometimes called "specialists." Each specialist kept the books on all buy and sell orders for a specific security at any price. If, for example, at any time during the trading day, the number of sellers heavily outweighed the number of buyers at any price that would be an orderly change from the previous trade price, then the specialist was expected to act as a "market maker" and buy on his/her own account to limit the decline in price to a small orderly change from the previous transaction price. If, on the other hand, the number of buy orders far exceeded the number of sell orders, then the market maker would sell from his/her own portfolio in order to maintain an orderly increase in price.

Orderliness is a necessary condition to convince holders of the market traded asset that they can readily liquidate for money their portfolio position at a market price close to the last publically announced price. In other words, orderliness is necessary to maintain liquidity in these markets.

Modern financial EMT suggests that these quaint institutional arrangements for market maker specialists are antiquated in this computer age. The computer can keep the book on buy and sell orders, and, it is claimed, the computer can match buy and sell orders and therefore maintain orderliness. With the computer and the Internet, there will be a meeting of huge numbers of buyers and sellers done rapidly and efficiently in virtual space. Consequently, there is no need for humans to act as specialists to keep the books and to assure the public that the market is well-organized and orderly.

Underlying this EMT of financial markets is the presumption that the value of traded financial assets is already predetermined by today's market "fundamentals" (at least in the long run).[3] Former

US Treasury Secretary and Harvard professor Lawrence Summers has written that financial markets are efficient in that their "ultimate social functions are spreading risks, guiding investment of scarce capital, and processing and disseminating the information possessed by diverse traders. ... *prices always reflect fundamental values* ... . The logic of efficient markets is compelling."[4]

In the numerous financial markets that failed in the winter of 2007–2008, the underlying financial instruments that were to provide the future cash flow for investors typically involved long-term debt instruments such as mortgages, or long-term corporate or municipal bonds. A necessary condition for these markets to be efficient is that the probabilistic risk of the debtors to fail to meet all future cash flow contractual debt obligations can be "known" to all market participants with actuarial certainty. With this actuarial knowledge, it even can be profitable for insurance companies to sell credit default swaps insurance to holders of these financial debt instruments guaranteeing the holder would be reimbursed for remaining interest payments and principal repayment at maturity if a default occurred.

In the EMT, any observed market price variation around the actuarial value (price) of the traded liquid assets representing these debt instruments in the aforementioned markets is presumed to be statistical "white noise." Any statistician will tell you, if the size of the sample increases, then the variance (i.e., the quantitative measure of the white noise) decreases. Since computers can bring together many more buyers and sellers globally than the antiquated pre-computer market arrangements, at any point of time the size of the sample of trading participants in the computer age will rise dramatically. If, therefore, you believe in the EMT, then permitting computers to organize the market will decrease significantly the variance and therefore increase the probability of a more well-organized and orderly market than existed in the pre-computer era.

Consequently, EMT advocates such as Summers suggest that the spreading of probabilistic risks for holders of these assets is much more efficient while the cost of each transaction is diminished significantly as computers take over from human order keepers. Underlying the EMT is a fundamental axiom: the ergodic axiom. This axiom presumes there exists an unchanged probability distribution governing past, present and future events. Consequently, available information on market fundamentals is represented by historical data. Only if the system is ergodic will this historical data provide useful information regarding future earnings, payments and so on. If one accepts the ergodic axiom, then as Summers states, "The logic of efficient market theory is compelling."

For believers in EMT, the presumption that, at any moment in time, there is a plethora of market participant buyers and sellers that can be collected by a computer assures that the assets being traded are very liquid. In a world of efficient financial markets, holders of market traded assets can readily liquidate their position at a price close to the previously announced market price whenever any holder wishes to reduce his/her position in that asset. If the EMT theory is applicable to our world, then how can we explain why in 2007–2008 so many securitized financial markets failed in the sense that "investors are finding themselves locked into investments they can't cash out of"[5]?

Keynes's LPT can provide the explanation. LPT presumes that the economic future is uncertain. Consequently, as we have already explained, the classical ergodic axiom[6] that is fundamental to any EMT is not applicable to real world financial markets. Keynes's analysis presumes that, in the real world of experience, the macro-economic and financial systems are determined by a nonergodic stochastic system. In a nonergodic world, current or past probability distribution functions are not reliable guides to the probability of future outcomes.

If future outcomes cannot be reliably predicted on the basis of existing past and present data, then there is no actuarial basis for insurance companies to provide holders of these assets protection against unfavorable outcomes. Accordingly, it should not be surprising that insurance companies such as AIG that wrote credit default swap insurance policies to protect asset holders against possible unfavorable outcomes found themselves experiencing billions of dollars more in losses than they had previously estimated.[7] In a nonergodic world, it is impossible to develop insurance premiums that will cover estimated insurance payouts in the future. Nor will there be available "fundamentals" data providing market participants with an actuarially correct outlook about the future value of these financial instruments.

In our world of (nonergodic) uncertainty, the primary function of financial markets that trade in resalable assets is to provide liquidity. The degree of liquidity of the assets traded in any organized market will be enhanced by the existence of a credible market maker. As previously stated, a market maker is someone who attempts to create public confidence in the belief that there will always be an orderly resale market. In other words, in a market where a market maker exists, holders of the asset can be reasonably confident that they can always execute a fast exit strategy and liquidate their position in the asset at a market price that is very close to the last publically recorded price. In essence, the market maker suggests to holders that if buyers do not appear to purchase offered securities at an orderly decline in price, then the market maker will make his/her best efforts to maintain orderliness even if this requires the market maker to buy, for his/her own account, the securities offered for sale. If the market maker cannot support his/her assurance to maintain orderliness with sufficient cash when a cascade of sell orders come onto the market, then the market will fail, and the asset becomes virtually illiquid as trading will be suspended until the market maker can rally enough additional support for the buyers' side of the market to reinstate orderliness. This temporary suspension of trading in a well-organized market that is orderly is typically called a "circuit breaker."

In other words, in our world of nonergodic uncertainty, for an orderly liquid resale market to exist *there must be a creditable "market maker"* who assures the public that he/she will swim against any rip-tide of sell (or buy) orders. The market maker must therefore be very wealthy, or at least have access to significant quantities of cash if needed. Nevertheless, any private market maker could exhaust his/her cash reserve in fighting against a cascade of sell orders from holders. Liquidity can be guaranteed under the most harshest of market conditions *only* if the market maker has easy direct or indirect access to the central bank to obtain all the funds necessary to maintain financial market orderliness. Only market makers having such preferred access to the central bank can be reasonably certain that they can *always* obtain enough cash to stem any potential disastrous financial market collapse.

An interesting illustration of this market maker exercise occurred on the days following the terrorist attacks on the World Trade Center and the Pentagon on September 11, 2001. As the World Trade Center buildings collapsed, there was a great fear that public confidence in New York financial markets and the US government would also collapse. To maintain confidence in the US government bond market, in the two days following the attack, the Federal Reserve pumped $45 billion into the banking system. Simultaneously, since the primary bond dealers in New York tend to "make" the US government bond market,

> to ease cash concerns among primary dealers in bonds – which include investment banks that aren't able to borrow money directly from the Fed – the Fed on Thursday [September 13, 2001] snapped up all the government securities offered by dealers, $70.2 billion worth. On Friday it poured even more into the system, buying a record $81.25 billion of government securities.[8]

In effect, these actions of the Federal Reserve removed securities from the general public by making the market and providing easily available liquidity to financial intermediaries. These intermediaries could then also make the market by purchasing all government bonds offered by members of the general public who wanted to make a fast exit.

Furthermore, *The Wall Street Journal* reported that just before the New York Stock Exchange reopened on September 17 for the first time after the World Trade Center attack, investment banker Goldman Sachs, loaded with liquidity due to Federal Reserve activities, phoned the chief investment officer of a large mutual fund group to tell him that Goldman was willing to buy any stocks the mutual fund managers wanted to sell. The *Journal* notes that, at the same time, corporations "also jumped in, taking advantage of regulators' newly relaxed stock buyback rules."[9] These corporations bought back securities that the general public had held, thereby making the market for their securities by propping up the price of their securities.

In another case, on March 13, 2008, the Federal Reserve worked out a deal via J. P. Morgan Chase to provide Bear Stearns with a loan against which Bear Stearns pledged as collateral its almost illiquid mortgage backed derivative securities. This permitted Bear to avoid having to dump its mortgage backed derivative securities onto an already set of failing markets in an attempt to obtain enough liquidity to meet Bear's "repo" loans obligations due on March 14. Accordingly, Bear had gained some breathing room and the selling pressure on financial markets was relieved. J. P. Morgan was the conduit for the loans to Bear because Morgan had access to the Federal Reserve's discount window and it was also supervised by the Federal Reserve. Bear did not have access and was not supervised by the Federal Reserve. Nevertheless, it was obvious on March 13 that if Bear Stearns failed and the collateral was insufficient to cover the loan, the Federal Reserve and not J. P. Morgan would take the loss.

On the (Sunday) evening of March 16, the Federal Reserve and J. P. Morgan announced that J. P. Morgan would buy Bear for the fire sale price of $2 per share. (Bear shares had closed at $30 per share on Friday March 14.) The Federal Reserve also agreed to lend up to $30 billion to J. P. Morgan to finance the illiquid assets it would inherit from the purchase of Bear. In essence, the Federal Reserve was acting similarly to the Resolution Trust Corporation (RTC) that dealt with the illiquid assets of insolvent Savings and Loan banks in the 1989 Savings and Loan insolvency crisis[10] by preventing the dumping of financial assets onto the market to obtain cash. The Federal Reserve's action saved J. P. Morgan from having to dump Bear assets on the market to try to obtain enough cash to meet Bear obligations.

The post September 11, 2001, activities of the Federal Reserve flooding the banking system directly and other financial institutions indirectly with liquidity vividly demonstrates that the central bank can either directly or indirectly make the market in financial assets by reducing the outstanding supply of securities available for sale to the general public. The public could then satisfy its increased bearishness tendencies by increasing its money holdings without depressing the spot market price for financial assets in a disorderly manner. Until, and unless, the public's bearishness recedes, the central bank and the market makers can hold that portion of the outstanding liquid assets that the public does not want to own.

In sum, although the existence of a market maker provides a higher degree of liquidity for the financial assets, this assurance could dry up in severe sell conditions unless the central bank is willing to take action to provide resources to the market maker or even directly to the market. If the market maker runs down his/her own resources and is not backed by the monetary authority central bank indirectly, the asset becomes temporarily illiquid. Nevertheless, the asset holder "knows" that the market maker is providing his/her best effort to search to bolster the buyers' side and thereby restore liquidity to the market.

In markets without a market maker, there can be no assurance that the apparent liquidity of an asset will not disappear almost instantaneously. Moreover, in the absence of a market maker, there is nothing to inspire confidence that someone is working to try to restore liquidity to the market.

Those who suggest that one only needs a computer-based organization of a market are assuming the computer will always search and find enough participants to buy the security whenever there is a large number of holders who want to sell. After all, in their theory, the "white noise" variation of buyers' and sellers' offers at prices other than the "equilibrium price" in efficient markets is assumed to be normally distributed. Hence, by assumption about the distribution of buyers and sellers around any possible price, there can never be a shortage of participants on one side or the other of financial markets.

With the failure of thousands of auction rate security markets in February 2008, it was obvious that the computers failed to find sufficient buyers. Moreover, the computers do not have funds and are not programmed to automatically enter into failing markets and begin purchasing when almost everyone wants to sell at, or near, the last market price. The investment bankers who organize and sponsor the securitized markets such as mortgage backed derivatives, auction rate securities and other exotic financial assets did not, and would not, act as market makers. These bankers often engaged in "price talk" before the market opened each day[11] to suggest to their clients what they believed the price range of today's market clearing price will likely be. These "price talk" financial institutions, however, did not put their money where their mouth was. They are not required to try to make the market if the market clearing price is significantly below their "price talk" estimate.

Nevertheless, there are many reports that representatives of these investment bankers had told clients that the holding of these assets "were 'cash equivalents.'" Many holders of these exotic securities believed their holdings were very liquid since big financial institutions such as Goldman Sachs, Lehman Brothers and Merrill Lynch were the dealers who organized the markets and normally provided the "price talk."

In an article in the February 15, 2008 issue of *The New York Times*, it was reported that:

Some well-heeled investors got a big jolt from Goldman Sachs this week; Goldman, the most celebrated bank on Wall Street, refused to let them withdraw money from investments that they considered as safe as cash. ... Goldman, Lehman Brothers, Merrill Lynch and other banks have been telling investors the market for these securities is frozen – and so is their cash.[12]

Obviously, up until then, participants in these markets believed they were holding very liquid assets. Nevertheless, the absence of a credible market maker has shown how these assets can easily become illiquid! Had these investors learned the harsh realities of Keynes's LPT, instead of being seduced by the dolce tones of EMT sirens, they might never have participated in markets whose liquidity could be merely a fleeting mirage. Should not US security laws and regulations provide sufficient information, so that investors can make such an informed decision?

FINANCIAL MARKETS AND REGULATION POLICY

The proper policy response to a financial market crisis similar to what occurred in 2007–2008 can be broken into two parts. First, what can be done to prevent future reoccurrences of this widespread failure of public financial markets? Second, what, if anything, can be done to limit any depressing effects of a credit crunch that has developed in these securitized financial markets which do not have market makers but where the public believed the holdings were "as good as cash"? The question of prevention is the easier of the two to answer.

According to the "What we do" web page of the US Securities and Exchange Commission (SEC; www.sec.gov): "The mission of the U.S. Securities and Exchange Commission is to protect investors, maintain fair, orderly, and efficient markets, and facilitate capital formation." The SEC web page then goes on to note that the Securities Act of 1933 had two basic objectives: "require that investors receive financial and other significant information concerning securities being offered for public sales, and prohibit deceit, misrepresentations, and other frauds in the sale of securities."

The SEC regulations typically apply to public financial markets where the buyer and the seller of an asset do not ordinarily identify themselves to each other. In a public financial market each buyer purchases from the impersonal market place and each seller sells to the impersonal market. It is the responsibility of the SEC to assure investors that these public markets are orderly.

In contrast, a private financial market would be where both the buyer and the seller of any financial asset are identified to each other. For example, bank loans are typically a private market transaction that would not come under the purview of the SEC. Normally, there is no public resale market for securities created in private financial markets. The issued asset from a transaction in a private market traditionally has been an illiquid asset where the lender has "skin in the game" and therefore will not make the loan unless reasonably assured that the borrower will repay the interest due and principal of the debt. And in case of default, the lender will have possession of sufficient collateral as well.

On its web page, the SEC also declares that: "As more and more first-time investors turn to the markets to help secure their futures, pay for homes, and send children to college, our investor protection mission is more compelling than ever." Given the current experience of contagious failed and failing public financial markets, it would appear that the SEC has been lax in pursuing its stated mission of investor protection. Accordingly, the US Congress should require the SEC to enforce diligently the following rules:

1. *Public notice of potential illiquidity for public markets that do not have a credible market maker.* In the last quarter of a century, large financial underwriters have created public markets which, via securitization, appeared to convert long-term debt instruments (some of them very illiquid, e.g., mortgages) into the virtual equivalent of high yield, very liquid money market funds and other short-term deposit accounts. As the newspaper reports that we have cited indicate, given the celebrated status of the investment bank underwriters of these securities and the statements of their representatives to clients, individual investors were led to believe that they could liquidate their position at an orderly change in price from the publically announced clearing price of the last public auction. Moreover, the triple A rating given by rating agencies such as

Standard & Poor to these securitized public market exotic assets added to the belief that these markets would always be very liquid.

This perceived high degree of liquidity for these assets has now proven to be illusionary. Purchasers might have recognized the potential low degree of liquidity associated with these assets if the buyers were informed of all the small print regarding market organization. In markets such as that for derivatives, although the organizer-underwriter could buy for their own account, they were not obligated to maintain an orderly market. Since the mandate of the SEC is to assure orderly public financial markets and "require that investors receive financial and other significant information concerning securities being offered for public sales, and prohibit deceit, misrepresentations, ... in the sale of securities," it is would seem obvious that all public financial markets that are organized without the existence of a credible market maker should be shut down because of the potential for disorderliness. Alternatively, at a minimum, information regarding the potential illiquidity of such assets should be widely advertised and made part of essential information that must be given to each purchaser of the asset being traded.

The draconian action suggested in (1) above is likely to meet with severe political resistance, as the financial community will argue that in a global economy, with the ease of electronic transfer of funds, a prohibition of this sort would merely encourage investors looking for higher yields to deal with foreign financial underwriters and markets to the detriment of domestic financial institutions and domestic industries trying to obtain funding.

In the next chapter we will propose an innovative international payments system[13] that could prevent US residents from trading in foreign financial markets that the United States deemed detrimental to American firms that obey SEC rules while foreign firms do not follow SEC rules. If, however, we assume that the current global payments system remains in effect, and there is a fear of loss of jobs and profits for American firms in the financial industry, then the SEC could permit the existence of public financial markets without a credible market maker as long as the SEC required the organizers of such markets to clearly advertise the possible loss of liquidity that can occur to holders of assets traded in these markets.

A civilized society does not believe in "caveat emptor" for markets where products are sold that can have terribly adverse health effects on the purchaser. Despite the widespread public information that cigarette smoking is a tremendous health hazard, government regulations still require cigarette companies to print in bold letters on each package of cigarettes the caution warning that, "Smoking can be injurious to your health." In a similar manner, any purchases on an organized public financial market that does not have a credible market maker can have serious financial health effects on the purchasers. Accordingly, the SEC should require the following warning to potential purchasers of assets traded in a market without a credible market maker:

> *This market is not organized by a SEC certified credible market maker. Consequently it may not be possible to sustain the liquidity of the assets being traded. Holders must recognize that they may find that their position in these markets can be frozen and they may be unable to liquidate their holdings for cash.*

Furthermore, the SEC should set up strictly enforced rules regarding the minimal amount of financial resources relative to the size of the relevant market that an entity must possess in order to be certified as a credible market maker. The SEC will be required to recertify all market makers periodically, but at least once a year.

To the extent that mutual fund managers who deal with the public wish to participate in financial markets that operate without a SEC certified credible market maker, then the fund manager must set up a separate mutual fund that only deals in such securities. These specific mutual funds must advertise in bold letters the aforementioned warning – and this warning must be repeated to every investor any time he/she makes an investment in these mutual funds as well as every time the investor receives a statement either electronically or by regular mail of his/her position in the specific mutual fund.

2. *Prohibition against securitization that attempts to create a public market for assets that originated in private markets.*

The SEC should prohibit any attempt to create a securitized market for any financial instrument or a derivative backed by financial instruments that originates in a private financial market (e.g., mortgages, commercial bank loans, auto purchase loans).

3. *Congress should legislate a 21st-century version of the Glass–Steagall Act.* The purpose of such an act should force financial institutions to be either an ordinary bank lender creating loans for individual customers in a private financial market or an underwriter broker who can only deal with instruments created and resold in a public financial market.

What can be done to mitigate the depressing consequences of another financial crisis that still might develop in the future despite the SEC change in the rules?

There are a number of policy steps that can be taken including (1) the creation of 21st-century equivalents of the Roosevelt era Home Owners' Loan Corporation (HOLC), if the financial crisis is the result of a large wave of defaults in home mortgages, and the George H. W. Bush Administration's Resolution Trust Company (RTC), to alleviate the US housing bubble crisis and to prevent potential massive insolvency problems, and (2) the need for massive infusions in cash for financial institutions that are too big to fail.

To a significant extent, the Federal Reserve through its "quantitative easing" (QE) policy has provided a version of providing massive infusions of cash for financial institutions and individuals. QE is an unconventional monetary policy of the central bank when liquidity problems and potential insolvency problems are preventing an economy from responding positively to ordinary monetary policy. QE involves the central bank buying significant amounts of financial assets, not only of government bonds but also, often, otherwise illiquid financial assets, such as derivatives from commercial banks and other private institutions, such as pension funds, and even from individuals. This buying of financial assets increases the prices of those financial assets and infuses the selling institutions balance sheets with cash and liquidity, thereby simultaneously increasing the money supply and preventing selling institutions from facing insolvency problems.

In this QE policy, from 2008 till October 2014 the Federal Reserve bought over $3.5 trillion of financial assets including derivatives to provide cash to large institutions which had significant amounts of these financial assets on their balance sheets. Without QE by the Federal Reserve, the market price of many financial derivatives would have collapsed to near zero, thereby threatening insolvency for those institutions and individuals holding significant amounts on the asset side of their balance sheets.

NOTES

1. Auction rate securities are financial assets backed by the long-term debts of corporations and/or municipalities, where the returns paid are reset at frequent intervals through auctions. These auctions provide the primary source of liquidity for holders who want access to cash quickly. In recent years, these auctions have failed and, consequently, holders have been unable to liquidate.
2. A credit default swap is where the seller will pay the buyer of the credit default swap if a specified debtor defaults on a specific loan. The buyer need not own the specific debt certificate of the debtor. Consequently, credit default swaps are often bought if one wants to bet that the debtor will default.
3. If the EMT is buttressed by the assumption of rational expectations, then expectations about the long run assure that short-run market prices do not get far out of line with their long-run "fundamentals" determined price.
4. L. Summers and V. Summers, "When Financial Markets Work Too Well: A Cautious Case for a Securities Transactions Tax," *Journal of Financial Services, 3*, 1989, p. 166, emphasis added.
5. J. J. Kim and S. Anand, "Some Investors Forced to Hold 'Auction' Bonds: Market Freeze Leaves Them Unable to Cash Out Securities that were Pitched as 'Safe,'" *Wall Street Journal*, February 21, 2008, p. D1.
6. In deterministic economic models the ordering axiom plays the same role that the ergodic axiom does in probabilistic efficient market models.
7. G. Morgenson, "Arcane Market Is Next to Face Big Credit Test," *New York Times*, February 17, 2008, p. A1.
8. A. Raghavan, S. Pulliam and J. Opdyke, "Team Effort: Banks and Regulators Drew Together to Calm Markets after Attack," *Wall Street Journal*, October 18, 2001, p. A1.
9. Op. cit., p. A1.
10. The need for a revived RTC to help solve the financial market crisis that was initiated with the subprime mortgage problem was emphasized in P. Davidson, "How to Solve the U.S. Housing Problem and Avoid Recession: A Revived HOLC and RTC," *Schwartz Center for Economic Policy Analysis: Policy Note*, January, 2008, online at: http//eco.bus.utk.edu/davidson.html.
11. Before the day's auction begins, the investment banker will typically provide "price talk" to their clients indicating a range of likely clearing rates for that auction. This range is based on a number of factors including the issuer's credit rating, the last clearance rate for this and similar issues and general macroeconomic conditions.
12. J. Anderson and V. Bajaj, "New Trouble in Auction-Rate Securities," *New York Times*, February 15, 2008, p. D4.

13. The proposed international payments system is a variant of the Keynes Plan that was presented by Keynes at the Bretton Woods conference in 1944 and rejected by the United States.

9. Globalization, international trade and international payments

Keynes's general theory explains that increases in spending on goods and services create additional profit opportunities for business firms. It follows that the managers of these business firms would be encouraged to hire additional workers whenever additional profit opportunities exist. In the closed economy model of most textbooks, where all transactions are among residents of the same national economy, it is implicitly assumed that the additional spending would come from domestic households, domestic business firms and/or federal, state or local governments to be spent to purchase the output produced by enterprises located in the domestic economy.

Once the analysis is placed into a globalized market system involving many separate nations things change somewhat. For example, spending by US households, business firms and/or government to purchase products produced in foreign nations (i.e., imports) creates profit opportunities and jobs in the foreign nation and not in the domestic economy. On the other hand, demand by foreigners for the products of domestically located business firms (i.e., exports) creates profits and jobs for workers in the domestic economy.

If, in any year, exports from the United States approximately equals the imports into the United States, then the foreign job creating effects of US imports and domestic job creation in US export industries will approximately offset each other. If, however, the US imports significantly more than it exports to foreigners, then American spending on imports will support more profit opportunities and jobs in foreign nations than foreigners' spending on US imports creates profit and job opportunities in the United States. In this latter case, American factories' profits and jobs will be less than if either the total imports equaled the level of exports or if all the United States' excess demand for imports over exports had been diverted to a market demand for these same products produced by domestically located production facilities.

For example, in 2008 the United States imported $709 billion more of goods and services from foreign nations than it exported to foreign markets. If that $709 billion that Americans spent for imports over exports had been spent in 2008 on goods and services produced in the United States, it would have had a big stimulus impact on the American economy that was then suffering from what some people called the Great Recession. This $709 billion was equal to approximately 95 percent of the amount of additional federal government spending and tax cuts provided for in the economic stimulus bill that President Obama signed in February 2009. This stimulus bill was supposed to end the Great Recession and restore jobs to several million US workers who had lost their jobs in this Great Recession.

Similarly, suppose the Chinese, Japanese and other trading partners who experience exports to the United States greater than imports from the United States had spent their 2008 total dollar earnings derived from their selling goods and services to people in the United States on exports from the United States instead of saving $709 billion of their export earnings. This additional $709 billion spending on US exports also would have been approximately 95 percent equivalent to the effect of the US federal government stimulus bill enacted in 2009 to alleviate the effects of the Great Recession. Accordingly, if a nation spends more on imports than it receives in exports, then the net effect is to reduce total market demand for the output from domestic industries and therefore to contribute to the market forces causing domestic unemployment while encouraging greater employment and profits abroad.

Since 1976, the United States has been consistently importing more than it has been exporting, thereby creating more profit opportunities and jobs in foreign nations than foreigners have been creating in the US export industries. The result has been that the United States has acted as the major engine for stimulus and economic growth for the rest of the world's industries for more than three decades. The impressive economic growth rates displayed by countries like Japan in the 1980s and China and India in the early years of the 21st century owe that prosperity in large part to the United States' increases in spending on exports from these nations.

A simple example will illustrate this situation. Let us assume that in any one year the United States spends $10 billion more on Chinese imports (say toys) and therefore $10 billion less on domestically produced toys. Assume that China does not increase spending on US exports and therefore the United States' trade deficit with China has increased by $10 billion. The effect is that this $10 billion spent on imports from China has created profits and jobs in the Chinese toy industry, while US residents who have diverted their spending on domestically produced toys to foreign produced toys have, in essence, destroyed profits and jobs in the United States' toy industry.

In this hypothetical example, China has earned $10 billion more dollars on its international trade payments account. It is further assumed that China did not spend this on buying $10 billion worth of more products from the United States. Instead, this hypothetical example has assumed China has "saved" $10 billion out of its international earnings. Since in the Keynes–Post Keynesian analysis "a penny saved is a penny that can not be earned" by anyone else, then in this hypothetical example the $10 billion the Chinese saved is $10 billion that cannot be earned by businesses and workers located in the United States. Former Federal Reserve chairman Ben Bernanke spoke of this foreign nations' hoarding of earnings from exports to the United States as a "glut of savings overseas."

When imports exceed exports for a nation, there is a deficit in the trade balance of that nation that economists call an "unfavorable balance of trade." In our hypothetical example of $10 billion that the Chinese saved, this unfavorable balance of trade results in a deficit in the United States' balance of payments with the rest of the world as the United States pays out more for its imports than it receives in payments for its exports.

Any nation experiencing a deficit in its international balance of payments must finance this deficit by either (1) the deficit nation drawing down its previous savings on international earnings (these savings are called the nation's "foreign reserves") to pay for its excess of imports over exports or (2) the deficit nation borrowing from foreigners in the rest of the world to pay for the difference between the value of imports and the value of exports.

Since the United States' imports have exceed exports every year since 1974, the United States, for many years, has borrowed from foreigners in order to finance its excess of imports over exports. The result has been that the United States has moved from being the world's largest creditor nation to being the largest debtor nation in terms of debt owed to the rest of the world.

To continue with our previous illustrative example, we might ask what the Chinese should do with the $10 billion savings on their international earnings? Like all savers, the Chinese look for liquid assets to move their saved (unused) international contractual settlement (purchasing) power to the future. For the most part, the Chinese have used their international savings to purchase US Treasury securities and other debt obligations of US government sponsored corporations. This indicates that the Chinese believe the US dollar is the safest harbor for storing their unused international contractual settlement power. These savings by the Chinese have led many classical theory "experts" to say that the Chinese have been financing the American consumer shopping spree and the resulting growth of US international debt. These "experts" have warned that if nations such as China stop buying US securities with their annual international savings out of earnings from exports to the United States, then American consumers could no longer afford to buy as many imports and they would have to reduce their purchases of Chinese made goods at retail outlets like Walmart.

If Americans did stop buying Chinese imports, just think how this will devastate the profits of Chinese firms and threaten the jobs of Chinese workers. The result could even cause political unrest in China. The Chinese Communist party enjoys popular support as long as it not only protects the nation from foreign enemies, but also continues to support economic actions that result in substantial improvements in employment and living conditions for all Chinese citizens. If Chinese exports were to decline, then Chinese unemployment might increase and living standards decline. That could induce demonstrations and political unrest in China. In other words, politically as well as economically it is unlikely to be in China's interest to stop financing America's huge imports from, over exports to, China.

If, in our simple illustration, we suppose the Chinese did not use their international savings to buy US Treasury bonds and instead spent the $10 billion on the products of American domestically located industries, the result would be that:

1.   in China there would be more products from American producers, perhaps such as meat, corn and wheat. If more of these food products were available in China they would strongly embellish and improve the standard food diet of the average Chinese worker.
2.   American businesses and their workers would earn more income and therefore not have to borrow from the Chinese to finance their large import purchases of Chinese goods.

The morale of this illustration is that if the Chinese bought goods from the United States instead of buying US Treasury bonds, then the Chinese government would make available goods that could improve Chinese real living standards while American workers would have more employment and enough income to afford all the Chinese imports they bought without the United States having to go into debt to the Chinese.

This simple illustration suggests that one engine of growth that a nation might try is to expand its exports to the rest of the world. If successful, such an export expansion-led growth policy will result in increasing profits for domestic firms, creating jobs for domestic workers. Moreover, the nation will become a creditor to other countries as it runs a favorable balance of trade. If, however, one country runs a favorable balance of trade, then other nation(s) must run an unfavorable balance of trade, resulting in a tendency to lose jobs and profits to the nation pursuing an export-led growth policy. Thus, as Keynes noted, if each nation tries to stimulate its economy by running a favorable balance of trade to increase domestic profit opportunities and employment then this "may lead to a senseless international competition for a favorable balance of trade which injures all alike."[1]

Keynes and his Post Keynesian followers have developed a solution for preventing a competition among nations to stimulate their economy via attempting to maintain a favorable balance of trade. This solution will end persistent trade imbalances that cause the nation(s) with an unfavorable balance of trade to lose profit and job opportunities while incurring huge international debts. What is required is some form of an institutional arrangement that prevents any trade imbalance among nations to persist.

In contrast, the classical efficient market theory solution to this trade imbalance problem is that the debtor nation must reduce its imports relative to its exports. One way this can occur is to have a free market in currency exchanges to solve the problem. The classical theory maintains that if the Chinese currency (the renminbi) was traded in a free flexible foreign exchange market, and if the United States ran an unfavorable balance of trade with the Chinese, then the demand for the Chinese currency would lead to it substantially increasing in value relative to the US dollar. As a result, the retail dollar price in the United States of Chinese goods would rise. American consumers would find that Chinese goods were so expensive in terms of dollars that they could no longer afford to buy very much from the Chinese. The rise in the consumer price level would adversely affect the real income and living standards of the average employed American worker. Thus Chinese exports to the United States would decline significantly.

In China, on the other hand, with the appreciation of the Chinese currency relative to the dollar, the Chinese would experience a decline in the renminbi price of US imports, and therefore they would buy more imports from the United States[2] as their real income and living standards improved.

If, however, the value of the US dollar declined relative to the Chinese currency, then as the retail dollar price of Chinese imports increased the rate of inflation in the United States as measured by the consumer price index would rise as such imports are a significant portion of the American consumer budget.[3]

If the Federal Reserve believes that its primary obligation is to fight inflation, then the Federal Reserve might ramp up its anti-inflationary policy and increase the domestic interest rate. A rise in interest rates in the United States would destroy some existing profit opportunities for American business firms and increase unemployment in the United States. The goal of the Federal Reserve's anti-inflation monetary policy would be to reduce the incomes of Americans sufficiently so that American households reduce their purchases of all goods and services including imports from China as well as products from American factories. In other words, the Federal Reserve's policy would try to dampen economic activity globally. If the Federal Reserve's anti-inflation policy is successful, then the decline in market demand will act as a break as Americans buy fewer goods (both domestically produced and imports) in the market. This reduction in imports would probably slow the appreciation of the renminbi relative to the dollar and thereby have some impact on reducing the measured rate of inflation over time.

In this depressing scenario, as Americans buy fewer Chinese imports, profits and jobs in China's export industries would be reduced, creating unemployment and potential political unrest in China. With lower incomes in China, the Chinese market demand for US exports should decline, resulting in fewer profit opportunities in American export industries made possible by the ongoing devaluation of the dollar. Clearly, such a possible scenario is neither good for the American nor Chinese workers and business firms.

Classical theory avoids this possible unpleasant scenario by assuming that with free efficient markets there will *always* be full employment of capital and labor in all trading nations no matter what changes occur in the exchange rate of currencies between nations. In other words, classical theory merely assumes away the possible unemployment problem that could occur in both America and China if the free market permits the US dollar to be devalued relative to the renminbi in order to end the United States' unfavorable balance of trade. In the long run, classical theory asserts, as a matter of faith rather than as empirical evidence, that there must always be full employment in all nations.[4]

Thus by loading the classical model with sufficient but unrealistic assumptions, classical theory resolves any potential trade deficit problem by merely invoking the magic of free markets for foreign exchange of currencies, in a world where the future is known – at least in the long run.

Some more pragmatic economists have noted that historically when exchange rates have been permitted to change relatively freely in the market the results have often been devastating for the nation. Consequently, some experts have advocated a foreign exchange market where a market maker actually fixes the exchange rate at some pre-announced level. As a result, very often economic discussions on the requirements for a good international payments system have been limited to this question of the advantages and disadvantages of fixed versus flexible exchange rates.

Experience gained since the end of the Second World War, however, plus Keynes's revolutionary liquidity analysis, indicate that more is required than merely deciding whether exchange rates should be fixed or freely flexible. A mechanism must be designed to adequately resolve any persistent trade and international payments imbalances that could occur whether the exchange rates are fixed or flexible. The mechanism should be designed not only to resolve these imbalance problems but also to simultaneously promote global full employment – rather than just assume global full employment will always occur. Such a mechanism is embedded in the Keynes Plan for international trade and payment imbalances.

THE BRETTON WOODS SOLUTION

In 1944, as the Second World War was winding down, the victorious Allied nations organized a conference at Bretton Woods, New Hampshire. The purpose of this Bretton Woods conference was to design a post war international payments system. Keynes was the chief representative of the UK delegation. In contrast to the classical view of the desirability of free exchange rate markets, Keynes's position was that there is an incompatibility thesis in the classical theory approach to international trade and finance. Keynes argued that permitting free trade, flexible exchange rates and free capital mobility across international borders can be incompatible with the economic goal of global full employment and rapid economic growth.

Keynes offered an alternative analysis to the classical approach to the problem. This alternative was the "Keynes Plan" solution, an arrangement that would make international trade and financial flow arrangements compatible with global full employment and vigorous economic growth while, when necessary, permitting nations to introduce controls on any flow of capital funds that were being sent across national boundaries.

Keynes argued that the "main cause of failure" of any traditional international payments system – whether based on fixed or flexible exchange rates – was its inability to actively foster continuous global economic expansion whenever persistent trade payment imbalances occurred among trading nations. This failure, Keynes wrote, can be traced to a single characteristic. I ask close attention to this, because I shall argue that this provides a clue to the nature of any alternative which is to be successful. It is characteristic of a freely convertible international standard that it throws the main burden of adjustment on the country which is in the *debtor* position on the international balance of payments – that is, on the country which is (in this context) by hypothesis the *weaker* and above all the *smaller* in comparison with the other side of the scales which (for this purpose) is the rest of the world.[5]

Keynes concluded that an essential improvement in designing any international payments system requires transferring the major *onus* of adjustment from the debtor to the creditor nation when any persistent international payments imbalance develops. This transfer of responsibility for ending persistent international imbalances to those nations that experience exports that exceed their imports and are therefore in the creditor position would, Keynes explained, substitute an expansionist, in place of a contractionist, pressure on world trade. To achieve a golden era of economic development, Keynes recommended combining a fixed, but adjustable, exchange rate system with a mechanism for requiring the nation "enjoying" a favorable balance of trade to initiate most of the effort necessary to eliminate this trade imbalance, while "maintaining enough discipline in the debtor countries to prevent them from exploiting the new ease allowed them."[6]

During the Second World War, millions of people were killed or wounded. Industrial and residential centers in most of Europe lay in ruins. Europe was on the brink of famine as agricultural production had been disrupted by the war. Transportation infrastructure was in a shambles. The war-torn capitalist nations in Europe did not have sufficient undamaged productive resources available to produce enough to feed their populations, and much less to rebuild their economies.

The only major economic power in the world that was not significantly damaged by the war was the United States. European rebuilding would require the European nations to run huge import surpluses with the United States in order to meet their economic needs for recovery. The European nations had very little foreign reserves. (At the time, the major foreign reserves were in the form of the asset gold that European war-devastated nations could readily sell to the United States for dollars that they could then use to buy imports from the only post war nation that had enough productivity capacity to produce for exports – the United States.)

The European nations had insufficient foreign reserves to obtain the necessary large volume of imports from the United States necessary to restore their economies. The only alternative, under a free market *laissez-faire* system, would be for Europeans to obtain an enormous volume of loans from the United States to finance the purchase of the US exports needed to feed the European population and rebuild their economies. Private sector lenders in the United States, however, were mindful that German reparation payments to the victorious Allied nations after the First World War were primarily financed by American private investors lending to Germany (the so-called Dawes Plan). Germany never repaid these Dawes Plan loans. Given this history of nations defaulting on international debt repayments and the existing circumstances immediately after the Second World War, it was obvious that private lending facilities in the United States could not be expected to provide the loans necessary for European recovery after the war.

The Keynes Plan, presented at the 1944 Bretton Woods conference, would require the United States, as the obvious major creditor nation, to accept the major responsibility for curing the post war trade imbalance, where a tremendous amount of goods from the United States would be necessary to feed the populations in Europe while simultaneously rebuilding the factories and infrastructure necessary to reestablish viable European economies.

Where were the Europeans going to get the finance to purchase all the necessary goods from the United States? Keynes estimated that the European nations might require in excess of $10 billion to purchase US exports for such a post war rebuilding of the European economies. The Keynes Plan had an operational system that would have the United States simply provide these funds to the Europeans. The United States' representative to the Bretton Woods conference, Harry Dexter White, stated that the US Congress would never provide the $10 billion that Keynes estimated was the minimum required funding. Instead, White argued, Congress might be willing to provide, at most, $3 billion as the United States' contribution to solving this post war international financial problem for rebuilding European economies.

The US delegation at the Bretton Woods conference was the most important participant. It was clear that nothing could be done unless the US delegation agreed to any plan that was developed at the conference. White had the US delegation veto the Keynes Plan. Instead, White provided a plan that set up the IMF and what we now call the World Bank.

The White Plan envisioned the IMF providing short-term loans to nations running unfavorable balances of trade. These loans were supposed to give the debtor nations time to rebuild their economic structure and then stop importing more than they were exporting. Then these debtor nations were to pay off their debt to the IMF using earnings from their exports exceeding their import purchases. Under the White Plan, the United States would subscribe a maximum of $3 billion as its contribution to the IMF lending facilities.

The World Bank would borrow funds from the free market. These World Bank funds would then be used to provide long-term loans for rebuilding capital facilities and making capital improvements initially in the war-torn nations and later in the less developed countries. When the new facilities were in place, it was assumed that sufficiently more goods could be produced and sold profitably. Then the nations would use the new income earned from the new facilities to pay off the World Bank loans. This White Plan suggested by the US delegation was basically the institutional arrangements adopted at the Bretton Woods conference.

Under this White Plan, international loans from the IMF or the World Bank were the only available sources for financing the huge volume of imports from the United States that the war-torn nations would require *immediately* after the Second World War. It turned out, however, that the IMF and World Bank together did not have sufficient funds to make loans of the magnitude needed by the European nations. But even if the IMF and the World Bank could have provided loans sufficient to meet the needs of the war-torn nations, the result would have been a huge international indebtedness of these nations. Paying off these immense debt obligations would require the European population to accept the main burden of adjustment by being willing to "tighten their belts."

This belt tightening statement is a euphemism for "austerity" to indicate that the debtor nations would have to dramatically reduce their consumption spending for imports and even goods produced domestically. Such a plan could be put into effect only by reducing the income of the residents of European nations so that they would buy less output from both foreign and domestic enterprises in order to pay the annual debt servicing charges. This suggested no significant improvement in the standard of living of Europeans for years to come. The result would so depress Europeans as to possibly induce political revolutions in most of Western Europe. Not inconsequentially, the "tighten your belt" policies also would have limited Europe as a possible large profitable market in the future for American exporters.

To avoid the possibility of many European nations facing a desperate electorate that might opt for a communist system when faced with the dismal future the White Plan offered, the United States developed an alternative plan in the hope that Communism would not spread west from the Soviet Union to the democratic European nations. In 1948, President Truman recommended Congress accept the Marshall Plan. Despite White's argument that the United States would not be willing to give more than $3 billion to solving this international payments problem, Congress approved the Marshall Plan which provided $5 billion in foreign aid in 18 months and a total of $13 billion in four years. (Adjusted for inflation, this $13 billion sum is equivalent to approximately $160 billion in 2014 dollars.) The Marshall Plan was essentially a four year *gift* of $13 billion worth of American exports to the war-devastated nations. The Marshall Plan required no repayment by the recipients of these funds – and hence no "belt tightening."

The 1948 Marshall Plan gifts gave the recipient nations a sufficient number of dollars to buy approximately 2 percent of the total annual output (GDP) of the United States each year for four years. Despite Americans giving away 2 percent of their national income per annum, there was no real sacrifice for American households associated with the Marshall Plan as the remaining income was significantly greater than pre-war levels. The United States' standard of living during the first year of the Marshall Plan was still 25 percent larger than it had been in the last peacetime year of 1940. American household income continued to grow throughout the Marshall Plan period.

The Marshall Plan funds created profit opportunities for American firms and jobs for US workers. Full employment was readily sustained immediately after the war ended, despite government military spending being significantly reduced, which by itself might have created some post war unemployment problems. Partially offsetting this reduction in government military spending was the

Marshall Plan fund's spending that created significant increases in employment in US export industries just as several million men and women were discharged from the United States' armed forces and entered the United States' civilian labor force looking for jobs.

For the first time in its history, the United States did not suffer from a severe recession due to a lack of spending immediately following the cessation of a major war and a reduction in military spending by the federal government. The United States and most of the rest of the world experienced an economic "free lunch" as both the potential debtor nations and the creditor nation experienced tremendous real economic gains resulting from the Marshall Plan and other foreign aid giveaways. Despite the growth in output from foreign factories, however, the United States maintained a surplus merchandise trade balance of exports over imports until the first oil price shock in 1973.

By 1958, however, although the United States still had an annual goods and services export surplus of over \$5 billion, the post war US potential international payments surplus was at an end. By that time US governmental foreign and military aid exceeded \$6 billion, while there was a net private capital outflow of \$1.6 billion from the United States that financed US companies investing in productive facilities abroad. This total of \$7.6 billion outflow of funds offset the earnings of the \$5 billion export surplus by \$2.6 billion. In other words, by 1958 the international payments account of the United States saw a net outflow of \$2.6 billion despite export earnings exceeding spending on imports by \$5 billion. The post war international payments surplus of the United States was at an end.

As the United States' total international payments account swung into deficit in 1958, other nations began to experience international payments surpluses. These credit surplus nations did not spend their payments surpluses on additional imports from the United States. Instead, the nations used a portion of their annual dollar surpluses to purchase international liquid assets in the form of gold reserves from the United States. For example, in 1958 the United States sold over \$2 billion in gold reserves to foreign central banks.

These trends accelerated in the 1960s, partly as a result of increased US military and financial aid in response to the construction of the Berlin Wall in 1961 and later because of the United States' increasing military involvement in Vietnam. At the same time, a rebuilt Europe and Japan became important producers of exports so that the rest of the world became less dependent on purchasing products solely from US export industries.

Still, the United States maintained a surplus merchandise trade balance of exports over imports until the first oil price shock in 1973. More than offsetting this merchandise trade surplus during most of the 1960s, however, were foreign and military aid dollar outflows to other nations plus net capital outflows from the United States that financed US companies investing in facilities abroad. Consequently, during the years of the 1960s the United States experienced an annual unfavorable total balance of international payments.

The Bretton Woods system had no way of automatically forcing the emerging creditor nations experiencing a payments surplus to step in and accept the responsibility for resolving the persistent international payments imbalances – a creditor adjustment role that contributed so wonderfully to global economic growth and one that the United States had started playing in 1948 with the Marshall Plan. Instead, during the 1960s the surplus nations continued to convert some portion of their annual dollar international payment receipt surpluses into demands on US gold reserves to be stored as a liquid asset for savings that could be used anytime in the future to meet international payments. As surplus nations in the 1960s drained gold reserves from the United States, the seeds of the destruction of the Bretton Woods system and the golden age of economic development were being sown.

In 1971, President Richard Nixon closed the gold window. Nixon stated that the US government would no longer sell gold to foreign nations who had earned dollars and wanted to use these dollars to buy gold from the United States rather than buy produced goods and services from American business firms. Nixon's closing of the gold window had, in essence, indicated that the United States had unilaterally withdrawn from any Bretton Woods agreement. At that point of time, the last vestiges of Keynes's enlightened international monetary approach, where the creditor nation accepts a large responsibility for correcting persistent trade imbalances, was on its way to being forgotten.

REFORMING THE INTERNATIONAL PAYMENTS SYSTEM

The post Second World War global golden age of economic development required international institutions and US government foreign aid policies that operated on principles inherent in the Keynes Plan where the creditor nation accepted the major responsibility for solving any persistent international payments imbalance. The formal Breton Woods agreement, however, did not require creditor nations to take such actions. Since Nixon's closing of the gold window in 1971, the onus has been on nations with deficits in their trade and international payments balances to solve their own international deficit payments problems. The result has been that since 1971 the international payments system often impedes rapid economic growth and has even induced recession for many nations of the world.

Utilizing the ideas Keynes presented at Bretton Woods, it is possible to update the Keynes Plan for a 21st-century international monetary payments scheme that would eliminate persistent unfavorable payments imbalances, promote global economic prosperity and still meet the political realities of today without bowing one's knee to efficient market advocates. For, as Keynes wrote:

> to suppose [as the classical theory does] that there exists some smoothly functioning automatic [free market] mechanism of adjustment which preserves equilibrium if only we trust to methods of *laissez-faire* is a doctrinaire delusion which disregards the lessons of historical experience without having behind it the support of sound theory.[7]

Since the 1990s, there have been several international finance crises. In 1994, when the Mexican government was faced with difficulties in trying to service its international debt repayments, some pragmatic policy makers recognized that free markets do not provide a system that automatically prevents a crisis in the international payments sector. In some cases, instead of relying on the market to solve the problem, these pragmatists advocated the creation of some sort of *crisis manager* to stop international financial market liquidity hemorrhaging and to "bail-out" the international investors. In 1994, for example, US Treasury Secretary Robert Rubin encouraged President Clinton to use American funds to lend to Mexico to solve its financial crisis and thereby save the wealth of international buyers of Mexican bonds. This solved the problem.

In other cases, when the solution was left to the free market, severe economic problems developed. In 1997, for example, Thailand, Malaysia and other East Asian nations experienced an international currency crisis that battered their economies. In 1998 the Russian debt default caused another international financial crisis that led to the collapse of the Long Term Capital Management (LTCM) hedge fund which, except for quick action by pragmatists at the New York Federal Reserve Bank, could have induced a significant drop in American equity markets. (We should note that among the principals of LTCM was Nobel Prize economist Myron Scholes, who won his Nobel Prize for discovering the formula for "properly" pricing risk in an efficient financial market environment. Scholes's formula, however, could not save LTCM from its after-the-fact recognized investment blunder into Russian bonds caused by not correctly pricing the risks involved in such an investment.)

At the time of the Russian debt default and the LTCM collapse, President Clinton called for a "new financial architecture" for international financial market transactions. The then IMF director, Stanley Fischer (who in 2014 Obama appointed as vice chair of the Federal Reserve), recognized that the IMF did not have sufficient funds to stem the international financial crises that were occurring. Fisher suggested that the major nations of the world, the so-called G7 nations, make a temporary arrangement where they would provide additional financing to help provide funds to any nation suffering from deficits in its international payments imbalances until such nations could get their economic house in order.

Fisher's cry for a G7 temporary collaboration to provide funds to deficit nations is equivalent to recruiting a volunteer fire department to douse the flames after someone has cried fire in a crowded theater. Even if the fire is ultimately extinguished, there will be a lot of innocent casualties. Moreover, every new currency fire would require the G7 voluntary fire department to pour more liquidity into the market to put out the flames. Clearly, a more desirable goal would be to produce a permanent fire prevention system and not to rely on organizing larger and larger volunteer fire fighting companies with each new currency crisis. In other words, crisis prevention rather than crisis management should be the policy goal.

President Clinton's clarion call for a new international financial architecture implicitly recognized the need for a permanent prevention institutional arrangement in the existing international payments system. Unfortunately, President Clinton's call was not taken up as the international community managed to muddle through the experience, although some nations and their residents suffered severe economic pains.

Beginning in 2007, the global economic system again experienced a crisis of the international financial system – a crisis of much larger proportions than those in the 1990s. The US subprime mortgage derivatives problem created a contagious disease that caused havoc with banking systems in many other countries including Germany, the United Kingdom, France, Spain, Greece and others. The contagion caused the almost complete collapse of the Icelandic banking system, and even the Swiss banking system – usually considered a paragon of financial stability – appeared for a while to be in severe economic trouble. The need for a "new international financial architecture" is clearly more urgent than ever.

In the 21st-century interdependent global economy, a substantial degree of economic cooperation among trading nations is essential. The original Keynes Plan for reforming the international payments system called for the creation of a single supranational central bank. Given the problems Europe has suffered despite it possessing a supranational central bank, this suggests that perhaps an institutional arrangement that avoids such a supranational central bank may be more desirable in that it permits participating nations to still manage their own monetary policy in the way the government thinks is in the best interests of its residents.

THE INTERNATIONAL MONETARY CLEARING UNION

An international financial architecture system to deal with persistent trade imbalances and any international financial crisis can be developed to operate under the same economic principles laid down by Keynes at Bretton Woods. But this system does not require the establishment of a supranational central bank of the world as Keynes suggested in his Keynes Plan at Bretton Woods. Instead, this new international payment system is aimed at obtaining a more acceptable international agreement (given today's political climate in most nations) that does not require any nation to surrender control of either its domestic banking system or the operation of its domestic monetary and fiscal policies to a supranational authority. Each nation will still be able to use monetary and fiscal policies to determine the domestic economic destiny that is best for its citizens as long as it does not detrimentally affect employment and income earning opportunities in other trading partner nations.

What is required is a closed, double-entry bookkeeping clearing institution to keep the international payments "score" among the various trading nations plus some mutually agreed-upon rules to solve the problems of persistent trade and international payment imbalances. It will also require an international agreement and a method to prevent international financial market transactions that can cause a financial market crisis that would be disruptive to the stability of any nation's economy as well as a threat to the global economy.

The new international institution to be set up under this plan could be labeled the International Monetary Clearing Union (IMCU). The IMCU would require all international payments between nations, whether for imports or financial funds crossing national borders, to go through this IMCU. Each nation's central bank would set up a deposit account with the IMCU. Then any payments of a resident entity in nation A made to a resident entity in nation B would have to clear through each nation's central bank deposit at the IMCU. A payment from a resident in A to a resident in B when cleared through the IMCU would appear as a credit for nation's B central bank account at the IMCU and as debit to nation's A central bank account at the IMCU. Although this may seem to be a complicated process to the average layperson, it is merely an international version of how checks are cleared when a resident of one region of the United States, say California, pays other entities in another region, say New York. The checks clear through the clearing house mechanism set up by the US Federal Reserve System.

This IMCU is a 21st-century variant of the Keynes Plan. To operate it would require at least seven technical proposals for dealing with all types of international financial problems that we have already indicated may occur. These technical proposals are presented in the appendix to this chapter. At this point, rather than letting the exposition get bogged down in technical details, it is more appropriate to indicate how and why this IMCU proposal works to end the possibility of persistent trade imbalances and disruptive flows of financial funds across national borders. Simultaneously, this IMCU would be encouraging global full employment and economic growth.

The object of this IMCU is:

1.   to prevent a lack of global effective market demand for the products of industry occurring due to liquidity problems whenever any nation(s) holds either excessive idle foreign reserves by saving (i.e., not spending on products) too much of its internationally earned income. In other words, this IMCU would encourage sufficient spending globally to produce enough profit incentives in export industries of nations to help assure global full employment;

2.   to provide an automatic mechanism for placing a major burden of correcting international trade imbalances on the nation running persistent export surpluses;

3.   to provide each nation with the ability to monitor and, if desired, control movements out of the nation of (a) flight financial funds, as well as money moved across national borders in order to avoid paying taxes on such funds, (b) earnings from illegal activities and (c) funds that cross borders to finance terrorist operations;

4.   to expand the quantity of the liquid asset used in settling international contracts (the asset of ultimate redemption) as global capacity warrants while protecting the international purchasing power of this asset.

The IMCU system would have a built-in mechanism to encourage any nation that runs persistent trade surpluses of exports over imports to spend what is deemed (in advance) by agreement of the international community to be "excessive" credit balances (savings) of foreign liquid reserve assets that have been deposited in the nation's deposit account at the IMCU. These accumulated credits (savings out of international earned income) represent funds that the creditor nation could have used to buy the products of foreign industries but instead used to increase its foreign reserves in terms of its deposit at the IMCU. When a nation holds excessive credits in its deposit account at the IMCU, it would mean that these excess credits are creating unemployment problems and a lack of profitable opportunities for business enterprises somewhere in the global economy.

The Keynes principle involved in this situation is to recognize that if the creditor nation spends its excessive credits, this spending will increase profit opportunities and the hiring of workers around the globe and thereby promote global full employment. The Keynes solution would encourage the creditor nation to spend these excessive credits in three possible ways – all beneficial to the global economy. These three ways are:

1. on the products (exports) of any other member nation of the IMCU;
2. on new direct foreign investment projects in other IMCU member nations;
3. to provide foreign aid, similar to the Marshall Plan, to deficit IMCU members.

The credit nation is free to choose any combination of the above three ways to spend its excessive credits at the IMCU, but it must spend its excessive credits.

If the creditor nation spends its excessive credits on imports from foreign producers, the result will be that the surplus nation's trade imbalance will be reduced while it is creating additional profits opportunities and labor hiring in other nations. This means more income for people and businesses in the nations previously experiencing unfavorable balances of trade and who were borrowing from foreigners to buy their excess of imports over exports. In essence, this excess credit spending on imports gives the deficit nations the opportunity to work their way out of international debt by earning additional income by selling additional exports to their creditors.

Direct foreign investment spending requires the nation with excess credits in its account at the IMCU to build plant and equipment in the deficit nation, thereby immediately increasing profits, jobs and income in the construction industries in the deficit nation and then creating jobs opportunities in manning the new plant and equipment when construction is completed. If the nation receiving this direct foreign investment is a less developed country, then this foreign direct investment spending helps to build the facilities of this less developed country up to 21st-century standards.

Foreign aid spending provides the deficit nation with a "gift" that it can use to reduce its debt obligations and/or buy additional products from foreign producers without going further into debt.

These three spending alternatives encourage the surplus nation to accept a major responsibility for correcting trade and international payments imbalances. Nevertheless, this provision gives the trade surplus country considerable discretion in deciding how to accept the onus of adjustment in the way it believes is in its residents' best interests. It does not permit, however, the surplus nation to shift the burden to the deficit nation(s) by lending the deficit nation or nations more and therefore imposing on any deficit nation additional contractual debt repayments obligations independent of what the deficit nation can afford.

The important thing is to make sure that continual oversaving by the surplus nation in the form of international liquid reserves are not permitted to unleash depressionary economic forces on other nations and/or to build up international debts so encumbering as to impoverish the global economy of the 21st century.

In the event that the surplus nation does not spend or give away the credits that are deemed "excessive" within a specified time, then the IMCU managers would confiscate (and redistribute to debtor members) the portion of credits deemed excessive. This last resort is the equivalent of a 100 percent tax on a nation's liquidity holdings that the international community has already agreed are excessive. Since continual excessive liquidity holdings implies continuing and excessive unemployment in one or more nations running trade deficits, if the surplus nation does not spend its excessive surplus, then confiscating these excessive credits and providing them to debtor nations will not only benefit the debtors but improve the global employment rate and output. Of course, the nation with excessive credits will recognize that these credits are subject to a 100 percent tax if not spent. It is therefore highly unlikely that this confiscatory tax will ever have to be enforced.

Under either a fixed or a flexible rate system with each nation free to decide how much it will import, some nations will, at times, experience persistent trade deficits merely because their trading partners are not living up to their means – that is, because other nations are continually saving (hoarding) a portion of their foreign export earnings rather than spending it on the products of foreign workers and enterprises. By so doing, these oversavers are creating a lack of global market demand for the products that global industries can produce.

Under the Keynes principle requiring creditor nations to spend excessive credits, deficit countries would no longer have to tighten their belts and reduce the income of their residents, in an attempt to reduce imports and thereby reduce their payment imbalance, because others are excessively oversaving. Instead, the system would seek to remedy the payment deficit by increasing opportunities for deficit nations to sell products profitably abroad and thereby work their way out of their otherwise deteriorating debtor position.

As the 2007–2008 global financial crisis deepened, some recognized that merely attempting to tinker with the existing system by perhaps upgrading the power of the IMF and the World Bank or encouraging the G7 to again act as a volunteer fire department did not solve the international trade and financial payments problems. For years now the international system has been running into trouble while patches to the existing IMF and World Bank system were applied in a vain attempt to end these global trade and payments problems. The world lost a great opportunity in 1944 when the United States vetoed the Keynes Plan at Bretton Woods. Let us hope we do not squander this opportunity again.

When the 2009 Obama recovery plan took effect, whatever economic recovery that the American economy experienced again placed the United States as the engine of growth for China and many other less developed nations. It tended to aggravate the United States' international payments imbalance problem as, after 2009, the United States began again to increase its imports by a greater amount than it is increasing the volume of exports. If this result continues, then, under the existing international payments system, the result may be to create an atmosphere where many fear the status of the dollar as the most liquid safe harbor foreign reserve asset. Such fears can only roil global financial markets and plunge the global economy into further crisis and recession.

If this were to occur, it should be even more obvious that a reform of the international trade and payments system is necessary if we are not to further aggravate any global economic crisis.

Hopefully, the leaders of the major nations will recognize the need to adopt some form of the Keynes Plan such as the IMCU if the global economy is ever to reinstate prosperous times for all the nations on earth.

THE CASE FOR CAPITAL CONTROLS

Since the future is uncertain, at any moment of time some event (ephemeral or not) may occur which can make residents of a nation feel more uncertain about the prospects of their economy. Under a system of free exchange markets, residents of the nation that fear the future can remove their savings from the domestic banking system and transfer them to another nation's banking and financial system where they believe the latter is a safe harbor to store their savings. The funds used in any attempt to find a safe haven in another nation is called "flight capital." If enough people try at the same time to move their funds from the domestic economy to this presumed safe harbor, the effect is similar to a run on a domestic bank that causes the bank to collapse.

In the case of bank runs, a policy of insuring deposits is usually sufficient to stop them occurring. Unfortunately, a cascade of flight capital fund movements out of a nation to a safe harbor in another nation cannot be stopped by merely insuring the deposits at domestic banks. Instead, this flight of funds if large enough can bring about the collapse of the domestic economy, as more and more people stop buying domestically produced goods to increase their holdings of foreign liquid assets. This creates significant recessionary pressures on the domestic economy thereby making it more difficult for the government to undertake economic policies to stabilize the nation's economy and prevent it from falling into recession or depression.

Since under the IMCU proposal all movement of funds across borders must go through the nation's central bank deposit at the IMCU, any nation can, if it desires, monitor and stop any cross border financial fund movements by merely refusing to allow the cross border banking transactions to be processed through the central bank's deposit on the IMCU's books. In other words, each nation can institute an effective policy to limit fund outflows from its country if, for any reason, the government deems it in the best interest of the nation's economy to prevent such fund outflows.

Thus, for example, if such a system was in place, the US government could, via a SEC ruling, prohibit the creation of domestic financial asset markets – such as mortgage backed derivatives – that are organized by investment bankers but do not have a reliable market maker institution to ensure orderliness and liquidity. Under this capital control provision, the American financial services industries would not have to fear the loss of customers and profits to foreign financial services firms who do not follow SEC rules when the SEC prohibits certain financial market activities by American financial services firms. The flow of funds could occur only if the foreign financial service firms agree to all the SEC rules required of domestic financial service firms. Thus the playing field would be level.

Finally, all movements of funds gained from illegal activities, or funds being moved from a country to another nation in order to avoid the domestic country's tax collector, or funds raised in one country that are being funneled to other countries to finance international terrorist activities, must also flow through the nation's central bank to the IMCU. Consequently, each nation has the facility, if it wishes, to monitor and if necessary stop such cross border money flow transactions from occurring. Clearly, this is an important aspect of the IMCU plan for it permits each nation to assure its citizens that others cannot take advantage of the international trading system to avoid paying their fair share of taxes, and to constrain the international financing of terrorist organizations, as well as to permit the government to undermine the profitability of any international illegal drug trade.

NOTES

1. J. M. Keynes, *The General Theory of Employment, Interest and Money* (Macmillan, London, 1936) pp. 338–339.
2. For technical reasons (known as when the Marshall–Lerner conditions are not applicable) that we need not discuss here, it is possible that even with a decline in the value of the US dollar relative to the Chinese renminbi, the value of the trade imbalance between China and the United States would not disappear and – in the worst case scenario – the trade imbalance between China and the United States could actually worsen. We will ignore this possible real world complication in the following discussion to illustrate other

possible deleterious effects of this classical theory solution to trade imbalances where free markets are suppose always to solve any trade imbalance problem by devaluing the currency of the country experiencing an unfavorable balance of trade.

3. If money wages of American workers did not increase, then the result of this classical theory solution would be to lower the standard of living of the average American worker until it approached the standard of living of Chinese workers.

4. And as endnote #2 indicates, mainstream economists assume away all possible economic problems.

5. J. M. Keynes, *The Collected Writings of John Maynard Keynes, 25*, edited by D. Moggridge (Macmillan, London, 1980) p. 27.

6. Op. cit., p. 30.

7. J. M. Keynes, "Post War Currency Policy," 1941, reprinted in *The Collected Writings of John Maynard Keynes, 25*, edited by D. Moggridge (Macmillan, London, 1980) pp. 21–22.

APPENDIX: THE TECHNICAL REQUIREMENTS FOR CREATING AN IMCU TO REFORM THE INTERNATIONAL PAYMENTS SYSTEM

There are seven major technical provisions in this IMCU system proposal. They are:

1. The unit of account and ultimate reserve asset for international liquidity will be the International Money Clearing Unit (hereafter IMC Unit). All IMC Units can be held *only* by the central banks of nations that abide by the rules of the clearing union system. IMC Units are not available to be held by the public.

2. Each nation's central bank, or, in the case of a common currency (e.g., the Euro), a currency union's central bank, will be committed to guarantee one-way convertibility from IMC Unit deposits at the clearing union to its domestic money to be used for the purchase of goods and services provided by domestic producers. Each central bank will set its own rules regarding making available foreign monies (through IMC Unit clearing transactions) to its own bankers and private sector residents.[1]

    Since central banks agree to sell their own liabilities (one-way convertibility) against the IMC Unit only to other central bankers via the IMCU while they simultaneously hold only IMC Units as liquid reserve assets for international financial transactions, there can be no draining of reserves from the international payments system. Ultimately, all major private international transactions clear between central banks' accounts in the books of the international clearing institution.

    The guarantee of only one-way convertibility permits each nation to institute controls and regulations on international capital fund outflows if necessary. The primary economic function of these international capital flow controls and regulations is to prevent rapid changes in the bull–bear sentiment from overwhelming the market maker and inducing dramatic changes in international financial market price trends that can have devastating real consequences.

    There is a spectrum of different capital controls available.

At one end of the spectrum are controls that primarily impose administrative constraints either on a case-by-case basis or an expenditure-category basis. Such controls may include administrative oversight and control of individual transactions for payments to foreign residents (or banks), often via oversight of international transactions by banks or their customers. Other capital controls might include the imposition of taxes (or other opportunity costs) on *specific* international financial transactions, for example, the 1960s' US Interest Equalization Tax.

Finally, there can be many forms of monetary policy decisions undertaken to affect net international financial flows, for example, raising the interest rate to slow capital outflows, raising bank reserve ratios, limiting the ability of banks to finance purchases of foreign securities, and regulating interbank activity. It has been argued that the 1997 East Asian currency contagion problem that almost brought down the global financial system was due to the interbank market that created the whirlpool of speculation. Mayer has stated that what was needed was "a system for identifying ... and policing interbank lending"[2] including banks' contingent liabilities resulting from dealing in derivatives. Recognizing the inability of economic models to correctly price risk in a nonergodic economic system, Mayer stated: "The mathematical models of price movements and covariance underlying the construction of these [contingent] liabilities simply collapsed as actual prices departed so far from 'normal' probabilities."[3]

The IMF, as lender of last resort during the 1997 East Asian contagion crisis, imposed the same conditions on all nations requiring loans for international liquidity purposes. The resulting worsening of the situation should have taught us that in policy prescriptions one size does *not* fit all situations. Accordingly, the type of capital regulation a nation should choose from the spectrum of tools available at any time will differ depending on the specific circumstances involved. It would be presumptuous to attempt to catalog what capital regulations should be imposed for any nation under any given circumstances. Nevertheless, it should be stressed that regulating capital movements may be a necessary *but not a sufficient* condition for promoting global prosperity. Much more is required.

If any government objects to the idea that the IMCU provision #2 provides governments with the ability to limit the free movement of "capital" funds, then this nation is free to join other nations of similar attitude in forming a currency union and thereby assuring a free flow of funds among the residents of the currency union.

3. Contracts between private individuals in different nations will continue to be denominated in whatever domestic currency permitted by local laws and agreed upon by the contracting parties. Contracts to be settled in terms of a foreign currency will therefore require some publically announced commitment from the central bank (through private sector bankers) of the availability of foreign funds to meet such private contractual obligations.

4. The exchange rate between the domestic currency and the IMC Unit will be set initially by each nation or currency union's central bank – just as it would be if one instituted an international gold standard. Since private enterprises that are already engaged in trade have international contractual commitments that would span the changeover interval from the current system, then, as a practical matter, one would expect, but not demand, that the existing exchange rate structure (with perhaps minor modifications) would provide the basis for initial rate setting.

   Provision #7 *infra* indicates when and how this nominal exchange rate between the national currency and the IMC Unit would be changed in the future.

5. An overdraft system will be built into the clearing union rules. Overdrafts will make available short-term unused creditor balances at the clearing house to finance the productive international transactions of others who need short-term credit. The terms will be determined by the *pro bono publico* clearing union managers.

6. A trigger mechanism will be created to encourage any creditor nation to spend what is deemed (in advance) by agreement of the international community to be "excessive" credit balances accumulated by running current account surpluses. These excessive credits can be spent in three ways: (a) on the products of any other member of the clearing union, (b) on new direct foreign investment projects and/or (c) to provide

unilateral transfers (foreign aid) to deficit members. Spending via (a) forces the surplus nation to make the adjustment directly by way of the trade balance on goods and services. Spending by way of (c) permits adjustment directly by the capital account balance, while (b) provides adjustment by the capital accounts (without setting up a contractual debt that will require reverse current account flows in the future).

In the unlikely event that the surplus nation does not spend or give away these credits within a specified time, then the clearing agency would confiscate (and redistribute to debtor members) the portion of credits deemed excessive.[4] This last resort confiscatory action (a 100 percent tax on excessive liquidity holdings) would make a payments adjustment via unilateral transfer payments in the current accounts.

In the absence of provision #6, under any conventional system, whether it has fixed or flexible exchange rates and/or capital controls, there can ultimately be an international liquidity crisis (as any persistent current account deficit can deplete a nation's foreign reserves) that unleashes global depressionary forces. Thus, provision #6 is necessary to ensure that the international payments system will not have a built-in depressionary bias. Ultimately then, it is in the self-interest of the surplus nation to accept this responsibility, for its actions will create conditions for global economic expansion, some of which must redound to its own residents. Failure to act, on the other hand, will promote global depressionary forces which will have some negative impact on its own residents.

7.   A system to stabilize the long-term purchasing power of the IMC Unit (in terms of each member nation's domestically produced market basket of goods) can be developed. This requires a system of fixed exchange rates between the local currency and the IMCU that changes only to reflect permanent increases in efficiency wages.[5] This assures each central bank that its holdings of IMC Units as the nation's foreign reserves will never lose purchasing power in terms of foreign produced goods. If a foreign government permits wage-price inflation to occur within its borders, then the exchange rate between the local currency and the IMC Unit will be devalued to reflect the inflation in the local money price of the

domestic produced goods and services. For example, if this rate of domestic inflation was 5 percent, the exchange rate would change so that each unit of the IMC Unit could purchase 5 percent more of the nation's currency.

If, on the other hand, increases in productivity lead to declining domestic production costs in terms of the domestic money, then the nation with this decline in efficiency wages (say of 5 percent) would have the option of choosing either (a) to permit the IMC Unit to buy (up to 5 percent) less units of domestic currency, thereby capturing all (or most of) the gains from productivity for its residents while maintaining the purchasing power of the IMC Unit, or (b) to keep the nominal exchange rate constant. In the latter case, the gain in productivity is shared with all trading partners. In exchange, the export industries in this productive nation will receive an increasing relative share of the world market.

By devaluing the exchange rate between local monies and the IMC Unit to offset the rate of domestic inflation, the IMC Unit's purchasing power is stabilized and inflation in one nation cannot be exported to another via the price of the first nation's exports.

By restricting the use of IMC Units to central banks, private speculation regarding IMC Units as a hedge against inflation is avoided. Each nation's rate of inflation of the goods and services it produces is determined solely by the local government's policy towards the level of domestic money wages and profit margins vis-à-vis productivity gains, that is, the nation's efficiency wage. Each nation is therefore free to experiment with policies for stabilizing its efficiency wage to prevent inflation as long as these policies do not lead to a lack of global effective demand. Whether the nation is successful or not in preventing domestic goods price inflation, the IMC Unit will never lose its international purchasing power in terms of any domestic money. Moreover, the IMC Unit has the promise of gaining in purchasing power over time, if productivity grows more than money wages and each nation is willing to share any reduction in real production costs with its trading partners.

Provision #7 produces a system designed to, at least, maintain the relative efficiency wage parities among nations.

In such a system, the adjustability of nominal exchange rates will be primarily to offset changes in efficiency wages among trading partners. A beneficial effect that follows from this provision is that it eliminates the possibility that a specific industry in any nation can be put at a competitive disadvantage (or secure a competitive advantage) against foreign producers solely because the nominal exchange rate changed independently of changes in efficiency wages and the real costs of production in each nation.

Consequently, nominal exchange rate variability can no longer create the problem of a loss of competitiveness due solely to the overvaluing of a currency as, for example, experienced by the industries in the American "rust belt" during the period 1982–1985. Even if temporary, currency appreciation independent of changes in efficiency wages can have significant permanent real costs as domestic industries abandon export markets and lose domestic market business to foreign firms, and the resultant existing excess plant and equipment is cast aside as too costly to maintain.

Provision #7 also prevents any nation from engaging in a beggar-thy-neighbor, export-thy-unemployment policy by pursuing a real exchange rate devaluation that does not reflect changes in efficiency wages. Once the initial exchange rates are chosen and relative efficiency wages are locked in, reduction in real production costs which are associated with a relative decline in efficiency wages is the main factor justifying an adjustment in the real exchange rate.

NOTES

1. Correspondent banking will have to operate through the IMCU, with each central bank regulating the international relations and operations of its domestic banking firms. Small scale smuggling of currency across borders and so on can never be completely eliminated. But such movements are merely a flea on a dog's back – a minor, but not debilitating, irritation. If, however, most of the residents of a nation hold and use (in violation of legal tender laws) a foreign currency for domestic transactions and as a store of value, this is evidence of a lack of confidence in the government and its monetary authority. Unless confidence is restored, all attempts to restore economic prosperity will fail.
2. M. Mayer, "The Asian Disease: Plausible Diagnoses, Possible Remedies," *Levy Institute Public Policy Brief No. 44*, 1998, pp. 29–30.

3. Op. cit., p. 31.
4. Whatever "excessive" credit balances are redistributed shall be apportioned among the debtor nations (perhaps based on a formula which is inversely related to each debtor's per capita income and directly related to the size of its international debt) to be used to reduce debit balances at the clearing union.
5. The efficiency wage is related to the money wage divided by the average product of labor; it is the unit labor cost modified by the profit mark-up in domestic money terms of domestically produced gross national product (GNP). At the preliminary stage of this proposal, it would serve no useful purpose to decide whether the domestic market basket should include both tradeable and nontradeable goods and services. (With the growth of tourism more and more nontradeable goods become potentially tradeable.) I personally prefer the wider concept of the domestic market basket, but it is not obvious that any essential principle is lost if a tradeable only concept is used, or if some nations use the wider concept while others the narrower one.

10. Is international free trade always beneficial?

One of the most widely believed policy conclusions of classical economic theory is that free trade among nations is beneficial in that it increases wealth and provides more goods and services for residents in all of the free trade nations. It consequently follows that all import and export markets should be made permanently free of any government regulations and/or restrictions such as tariffs or quotas. Nations such as the United States should pursue free trade agreements with all other nations on the globe. What is the classical theory basis for such a conclusion?

TRADE, THE WEALTH OF NATIONS AND THE LAW OF COMPARATIVE ADVANTAGE

The classical theory's "law of comparative advantage" is claimed to be a universal applicable truth that assures free trade produces more goods and services globally as all resources in every nation are fully employed in their most comparative productive capacity. This is accomplished by each nation specializing in producing and exporting from the domestic industries that have a "comparative advantage."

Comparative advantage associated with any nation's industry is determined by supply side relationships regarding the productivity of capital and labor in the specific production process. Any government interference with a free trading relationship between nations following the law of comparative advantage, it is claimed, will prevent the economic prosperity of the nations involved from reaching their potential optimal production solution.

Adam Smith,[1] on the other hand, believed that the ability of any nation to produce additional income and wealth is constrained primarily by the extent of demand in the market place and not supply side limitation conditions. By expanding the market for goods, Smith argued, the introduction of trade between nations permitted entrepreneurs to take advantages of the production economies of scale, thereby producing more from each worker employed and enhancing the income and the wealth of the nation. For Adam Smith, economic growth was primarily demand driven. The key is the expansion of market demand. An obvious moral of Smith's analysis is that no nation that aspires to be wealthy can be an island unto itself. Instead, it must expand production via export market demand for the products of its industry that have a comparative advantage.

Implicit in the Smith analogy is that consumers in the domestic market for the products of domestic industries are already satiated with the goods and services produced so that domestic market expansion for these domestic produced goods is not possible. In any case, supply constraints have no significant role to play in Smith's inquiry into what limits the wealth of nations at any point of time.

In 1819 the classical economist David Ricardo developed the concept of the law of comparative advantage to justify the importance of free trade among nations. Since Ricardo, advocates of international free trade have invoked the need for each nation to specialize in the domestic industry (industries) that has a comparative advantage in order to increase income and wealth in the face of supply constraints. Unlike Smith's argument, this Ricardian need for industry specialization to increase the wealth of nations does not rely on expanding market demand to be able to capture the economies of scale in domestic production. In a Ricardian world of trade, production in each nation occurs in the realm of diminishing returns, where the additional volume of goods produced by hiring an additional worker in a domestic industry is less than the addition to output produced by this last additional worker hired. In Ricardo's scheme, increases in aggregate domestic market demand will not, per se, lead to significant increases in the growth of the wealth by nations, especially in the face of diminishing returns which result in rising production costs per additional unit of output.

Rather, an increase in the wealth of trading nations depends on the law of comparative advantage determining the geographical location of industries and the resulting trade patterns between nations. Under this classical theory law of comparative advantage, nation A should specialize in that industry (industry #1) for which it has the greatest productivity and therefore cost advantage compared to the production costs of the same industry located in other nations, even if nation A has an absolute production cost advantage in industry #2 where nation B has a comparatively smaller cost disadvantage in industry #2 compared to industry #1. Nation A should concentrate its resources on production in industry #1, producing all that the domestic market demands and exporting to nation B all the product of industry #1 that the residents of nation B demand in the market. Nation B should concentrate its resources on industry #2 to meet all domestic demand plus export to nation A all they demand for the product of industry #2. The resulting geo-graphical industry location pattern and export–import pattern between these nations, the law of comparative advantage claims, permits the income and wealth of both trading nations to be better than if each nation domestically produced products from both industries solely for domestic consumption.

In Ricardo's time, a nation's comparative advantage was typically associated with its unique supply environment (e.g., availability of minerals deposits, climate differences and its effects on agricultural production) that resulted in differences in production costs. This comparative advantage argument for "free" trade is based on the notion of opening the domestic market to a foreign source which has lower costs of production due to *supply productivity advantages not available in the domestic economy.*

In Ricardo's famous wine–cloth example, it was the climate that gave Portugal its absolute as well as comparative advantage in production cost in grapes and wine. If the cost of labor in Portugal was much lower than in England in the mass production of cloth, then Portugal would have an absolute cost advantage in the production of cloth as well as wine. Nevertheless, the law of comparative advantage would argue that all the cloth for the market in both countries should be produced in England, while Portugal produced all the wine for both countries.

Even if the production of both wine and cloth per unit of output was cheaper in Portugal than England, it would be beneficial for Portugal to concentrate its resources in the production of grapes and wine where it had the greatest productivity cost advantage. Simi-larly, even though it cost more to produce wine and cloth in England, the latter should use its resources in the production of cloth, where it had the least cost disadvantage, rather than in producing grapes and wine where the relative cost disadvantage was greater.

The result would be a greater total production of wine and cloth for the same number of man hours worked in the two nations than if each nation produced both wine and cloth. This total supply increase due to free trade would make possible an increase in the quantity of wine and cloth available to consumers in both nations.

In Ricardo's time, agricultural products and minerals represented a very large share of total international trade. Divergences in production costs among nations due to climate and the nonrandom geographical distribution of natural resources were obviously significant. This meant that certain products were relatively cheaper to produce in one country than another. Consequently, Ricardo's law of comparative advantage was largely applicable for explaining free trade patterns between nations existing in the 19th century.

With the growth of mass production industries, however, the geographical location of industrial production is often determined on a different basis. In mass production manufacturing industries, differences in production costs among nations are not normally reflective of differences due to nature's climatic or mineral endowment associated with nation A vis-à-vis nation B. In mass production industries, the same technology typically is used in production of any particular product at any geographical location. Differences in costs across nations in these industries are primarily due to differences in wages and fringe benefits paid in one nation compared to the wages and fringe benefits in another.

Keynes recognized this possibility when he wrote

A considerable degree of international specialization is necessary in a rational world in all cases where it is dictated by wide differences in climate, natural resources ... . But over an increasingly wide range of industrial products ... . I become doubtful whether the economic costs of national self-sufficiency is great enough to outweigh the other advantages of gradually bringing the producer [worker] and the consumer within the ambit of the same national, economic and financial organization. Experience accumulates to prove that most modern mass-production processes can be performed in most countries and climates with equal efficiency.[2]

Today's facts demonstrate that, given the existence of multinational firms and the ease with which they can transfer technology internationally, any differences in relative costs of production in any particular industry is more likely to reflect national differences in money wages (per hour of labor), plus the costs of providing "civilized" working conditions, such as a safe and healthy environment for workers and limiting the use of child labor, plus the costs to the enterprise of providing health insurance and pension benefits for employees and so on. Today, in any free trade international system, where mass manufacturing and service industries are a major portion of total trading volume among nations, global industrial trade patterns are more likely to reflect differences in wages, occupational safety and other labor expenses that the enterprise must bear, rather than real costs associated with either national differences in climate or differences in the availability of natural resources.

In the 21st century, low transportation and/or communication costs have made the delivery costs in providing many goods and services to distant foreign markets very low. Consequently, mass production industries that use low skilled workers, semi-skilled workers or even, if available, high skilled workers are likely to locate in those nations where the economic system values human life the lowest, at least as measured by the wage paid per hour of labor and the work environment. Long ago most developed nations passed civilizing legislation that made unsafe "sweatshop" workshop conditions and the use of child labor illegal. Yet such conditions typically still exist in the competitive industries of most less developed nations. Consequently, the promotion of free trade competition among mass production industries favors the industries that have little or no regulations regarding sweatshop conditions, child labor use, low wages and so on. This means that in developed nations with high paid workers and civilized workplace rules, free trade threatens the economic lives and welfare of workers and their families as production can be outsourced and domestic unemployment problems become more prevalent and wages stagnate or even decline.

On the other hand, in those domestic production processes where communication and/or transportation costs are very high (e.g., personal services such as servants, waiters and barbers), and immigration legislation limits the importation of cheap labor, there cannot be any significant free trade foreign competition with domestic places of employment. Significant employment opportunities can still exist in these personal service industries of developed nations even though legislative regulations exist which require civilized working condition standards, minimum wages and so on. Nevertheless, if free trade outsourcing displaces a growing number of workers from previously high paying mass production industries in developed nations, then the competition for the existing personal service jobs in nontradeable production processes by these displaced workers is likely to depress wages[3] in these activities, or at least prevent the wage of employed workers from rising significantly over time. It is, therefore, no wonder that the share of wages in US GDP has been declining in recent decades as the United States has engaged in more free trade relationships with nations that continue to have sweatshops that have "equal efficiency" but are manned by low paid workers.

As we crossed the threshold into the 21st century, Keynes's analytical framework indicated that the argument for complete free international trade as a means of promoting the wealth of all nations and their inhabitants cannot be rationalized on the basis of the law of comparative advantage. Comparative advantage perhaps still exists for minerals, agriculture and other industries where productivity is related to climatic conditions or mineral availability. Production in these climate and natural resource related industries, however, is often controlled by the market power of cartels and/or producer nations' governmental policies designed to prevent market prices from falling sufficiently to just cover the "real" costs of production associated with climate or natural resource availability. Those industries for which the law of comparative advantage might still be applicable are often largely sheltered from international competitive forces by cartel or government power. These industries reap monopoly rents over and above the normal competitive return on their production.

In the production of oil, for example, since the 1970s the Organization of the Petroleum Exporting Countries (OPEC) cartel has created and maintained a large difference between the market price for crude oil and the costs of producing oil in countries such as Saudi Arabia and other Middle Eastern nations. Consequently, the profits to the OPEC cartel, including what economists call "monopoly rents," have, for decades, been very large. This cartel maintained a price that was so much greater than the potential cost of producing oil from shale that American and Canadian enterprises have had an incentive to find ways to develop the technology for production of oil from shale and still make a significant, more-than-competitive profit at the world price supported by the OPEC cartel. This new competition from shale oil has tended to reduce the cartel's control over the price of oil significantly in recent years, even though the price may be still much greater than the costs of production from oil wells in countries in the Middle East such as Saudi Arabia.[4]

The growth of multinational corporations in mass production industries and the movement towards a more liberalized free trading system in the final decades of the 20th century encouraged business enterprises in developed nations to transfer their production technology in order to "outsource" production, that is, to search for the lowest wage foreign workers available in order to reduce production costs. The availability of "outsourcing" to cheap foreign labor also acts as a countervailing power to the high cost for domestic workers organized by labor unions in developed countries.

Indeed, in the early years of the 21st century, the rapidly developing industrial structure of many nations (e.g., China, India, Southeast Asia) can be largely attributed to the competitive search by multinational firms to utilize low wage foreign workers to compete with the high wage workers in developed nations to produce identical goods and services under the same technological production processes. As suggested in Chapter 7, this outsourcing search for cheap foreign labor has created the equivalent of an "industrial reserve army" of foreign workers that has constrained and sometimes even reduced the wages and living standards of workers in developed nations.

In the early decades after the Second World War, when transportation and communication costs between nations was still significantly large, there were also national government restrictions regarding tariffs and import quotas. In this environment, labor unions in mass production industries in developed economies could easily obtain increasingly high wages for the unionized workers. This brought about increasingly high domestic unit labor costs in developed nations, which acted as a spur to encourage corporate managers to search for innovative domestic investment ways to improve domestic labor productivity and thereby reduce labor costs per unit of output. With the growth of multinationals and the removal of many restrictions on the international trading of mass produced manufactured goods, high domestic labor costs now are more likely to encourage managerial practices such as outsourcing, rather than encouraging investment in research and development to provide productivity enhancing new technology to lower unit labor production costs. Under current conditions, it is cheaper to out-source using existing technical production processes overseas then incur the higher cost of searching for further technological improvements in production processes to reduce unit production costs in developed nations. Consequently, the larger profits attributable to outsourcing have not been plowed back into research and technological development even if, in the long run, it is technological improvements that raise overall living standards.

Under the rules of free trade today, there is less of an incentive for managers to pursue innovations to improve domestic labor productivity in any mass production industrial sector as long as inexpensive foreign labor can "do the job" with the existing technology and transportation and/or communication costs, which are relatively small. The decline in the rate of growth of domestic labor productivity in many developed nations since the 1970s can be, at least partly, related to this phenomenon of emphasizing the use of cheap foreign labor vis-à-vis the search for domestic production process improvements by the private sector.

Except for production of some minerals and agricultural products, Post Keynesian analysis suggests that justification for the desirability of the expansion of international trade must be the result of increasing market demand globally. Demand driven expansion of trade can explain the growth of the wealth of nations in both the Adam Smith sense of exploiting economies of scale and in the sense of John Maynard Keynes who saw the lack of effective market demand as the main reason for the inability of economies to provide the full employment of resources income flow that they were capable of providing.

Nevertheless, rather than arguing that trade provides the opportunity for all nations to expand the effective market demand for the products they produce, defenders of free trade policies continually bring out the old chestnut of the classical theory's "law of comparative advantage" to justify "outsourcing" production by multinational firms in developed economies. These supporters of outsourcing claim that despite the obvious loss of the high wage jobs of American mass production workers to lower wage foreign workers, outsourcing is beneficial to both the US economy and the rest of the world. They argue that, in the long run, free trade will result in more income and wealth for all nations by creating new higher value production jobs for workers in the developed nations as well as the jobs created in the nations to which production has been outsourced.

Unfortunately, the claim that outsourcing and free trade will create new high valued jobs in developed nations requires at least two classical assumptions that are not readily applicable to the real world in which we live. First, it is assumed that the hypothesized additional high value product that will be supplied as workers move from the outsourced production lines to the more (unspecified) higher valued product production automatically will create its own additional global demand for these additional high valued products. This assertion that additional supply always creates its own additional market demand implies the applicability of Say's Law to the classical trade theory analysis. But as we have already noted, Keynes demonstrated that Say's Law could not be applied to money using, entrepreneurial economies. Full employment is not an automatic outcome of free market competition domestically or internationally. Consequently, if there is anything economists should have learned since Keynes, it is that one cannot prove that there will automatically be gains from free trade to be shared by all trading economies unless one can be assured that there is full employment in all nations – before and after free trade.

That brings us to a second assumption required to make Ricardo's law of comparative advantage applicable to the real world in which we live. The textbook comparative advantage analysis assumes that the gains from trade occur only if neither capital nor labor are mobile across national boundaries. If there is no capital or labor mobility across national boundaries, then the capital rich (developed) nations will specialize in industries that are most productive with a very capital intensive use of technology, while the less developed region that has plenty of labor but little capital specializes in the labor intensive industries. This trade pattern of comparative advantage will use capital and labor in industries where the technology makes them most productive and therefore, by assumption, the total output globally will be maximized.

If capital is internationally mobile, however, and if, after trade, there is not global full employment, then these hypothetical benefits from free trade need not occur. With free international capital mobility and free trade, entrepreneurs will locate technologically advanced plant and equipment investments to produce goods in those nations where it is most profitable to produce, that is, where unit labor and workshop condition costs are lowest.[5] Thus, if multinational firms can shift technology from nation to nation, then it will take the same number of man hours of input to produce a unit of output in each country – or as Keynes wrote, "modern mass production processes can be performed in most countries ... with equal efficiency."[6] Then the nation with cheap labor via lower money wage rates will have lower unit money labor costs for the production of manufactured items at all relevant ranges of production that the global market can absorb. As long as the less developed nation has an almost unlimited supply of cheap labor, the nation can attract enough foreign capital ultimately to produce all the manufactured goods necessary to meet global demand. In other words, as long as production with the latest technology does not run into significant diminishing returns and total after-trade demand is not sufficient to assure global full employment, international production and trade patterns of mass production goods will be determined solely by the absolute advantage of having a large supply of low money wage workers available. The result will be that employment and living standards of workers in developed nations will decline substantially.

Accordingly, the use of the classical comparative advantage analysis as a justification for letting free markets determine outsourcing, trade and international payments flows can be dangerous to the health of economies of developed nations, especially those that restrict the use of child labor, provide their workers with civilized working conditions and simultaneously provide a high wage standard of living. Such civilized nations will not have any absolute cost advantage in the production of tradeable goods and services vis-à-vis nations where child labor and low wages prevail.

In sum, if capital is mobile internationally, as long as the less developed nations have an absolute labor cost advantage in mass producing all tradeable goods because they have available a large additional supply of both unskilled and skilled cheap labor, then the classical theory justification in claiming free trade provides gains from trade for all nations is not applicable. Given abundant available cheap labor supply of unskilled and skilled workers, the less developed nations will attract foreign capital from the OECD nations to employ the cheap labor to produce most, if not all, the tradeable goods and services that can be profitably sold globally. The developed nations will be left mainly with employment in industries that produce goods and services that are not tradeable across national boundaries.

Of course, the proponents of free trade have an almost religious belief that despite the loss of high wage manufacturing jobs in developed nations due to outsourcing over recent years, the developed nations will develop (yet unspecified) higher skilled jobs in some advanced technology sector. The labor force in countries such as China and India will not have sufficient skills or education to be competitive in this forthcoming new technology high value product sector. Thus, the often heard comment that, in the long run, outsourcing is good for the developed economies with high cost labor forces, assumes that unemployment will not be a significant problem as new, still unforeseen higher skilled jobs will miraculously appear in developed nations such as the United States.

Why then have the displaced American workers chronicled by Uchitelle[7] not found these new high value jobs that free trade advocates argue must be coming to America? The conventional wisdom is that it is the displaced workers' own fault for their being eligible only for lower paying, less value productive jobs. An unemployed worker or a displaced worker needs only to pursue more education and they will always get a better job we are told, without a smile on the face of the perpetrator of this innocent fraud! A call for better-educated workers as the remedy for workers displaced by outsourcing is a measure of a mind that has not thought through the problems of trade patterns in a freely trading global economy where child labor, unsafe working conditions, environmentally damaging production and a host of other factors are devastating to the progress of a good civilized society.

Unless the governments of developed nations take deliberate action to secure and maintain full employment in their domestic economies, free trade has the potential to impoverish a significant portion of the population as unemployment rates in the these countries remain high and those workers who are employed are forced to accept a real wage that is closer to being competitive to wages being paid to the abundant supply of unskilled and skilled workers in cheap foreign labor countries. Surely, politicians in developed nations should be made aware of these potential "disastrous" results that can occur from blindly applying the classical theory explanation of the benefits of free trade to today's problem of job outsourcing.

NOTES

1. A. Smith, *An Inquiry into the Wealth of Nations* (1776) reprinted in 1937 by Modern Library, New York.
2. J. M. Keynes, "National Self Sufficiency," 1933, reprinted in *The Collected Writings of John Maynard Keynes, 21,* edited by D. Moggridge (Macmillan, London, 1982) p. 238.
3. L. Uchitelle, *The Disposable American: Layoffs and Their Consequences* (Knopf, New York, 2006).
4. This possibility was recognized in 1974 in a paper by P. Davidson, L. H. Falk and H. Lee, "Oil: Its Time Allocation and Project Independence," *Brookings Papers on Economic Activity, 2,* 1974. This paper is reprinted in *Inflation, Open Economies, and Resources: The Collected Writings of Paul Davidson, 2,* edited by L. Davidson (New York University Press, New York, 1991). The reference to shale is provided on p. 331 of the reprint edition.
5. Assuming transportation costs do not completely offset the lower labor costs per unit.
6. Op. cit., p. 238.
7. L. Uchitelle, *The Disposable American: Layoffs and Their Consequences* (Knopf, New York, 2006).

11. Policies to assure a civilized capitalist economic system

A civilized society should encourage its citizens to excel in all the endeavors they undertake. A civilized society must also provide its citizens with the opportunities to work. A civilized society should also encourage the productive members of the community to maintain a sensitivity and compassion for the needs of others and to have open and honest contractual dealing with everyone. All these objectives are easier to obtain in a capitalist economic system where everyone has the opportunity to work and earn income. The ability to earn an honest day's income for an honest day's work creates self-esteem for the employed person and all the members of his/her household. Accordingly, government policies should be designed to assure a profitable full employment economy.

For almost the last four decades, however, the public debate over economic policy has been dominated by the belief that if self-interested individuals are permitted to operate in a free market without government interference and regulation, and without worrying about other members of the community, the resulting free market will bring about an economic Utopia. Yet the terrible 2007–2008 global financial crisis resulted from deregulating financial institutions while permitting self-interested mortgage originators to encourage subprime borrowers to obtain a mortgage for a home they could not afford. Self-interested investment bankers then securitized these mortgages to subprime borrowers with a mix of more conventional mortgages and sold these mortgage backed derivatives with what later proved to be fraudulent claims that these derivative securities were as good as cash in terms of their liquidity. The result was a disaster not only to many home owners, who later found they could no longer afford their mortgage payments, but also to the many innocent people who lost jobs as the global economy sank into the Great Recession.

The purpose of this book has been to indicate that there is an alternative to the classical economic theory that (1) claimed that free markets are always the only way to make the economy beneficial to all members of society and (2) promoted the financial deregulation and the resulting market activity that brought on the Great Recession. This alternative Keynes–Post Keynesian theory provides a more realistic explanation of the operation of the market oriented entrepreneurial system in which we live. This alternative explanation also can provide guidelines on how to cure the flaws that remain in this market oriented entrepreneurial system without destroying the good things that are delivered by our economic system. The preceding chapters have explained how Keynes's explanation of the operation of our economic system indicates that government can and must assure that private sector employers have sufficient profit incentives to employ all workers who are actively seeking employment.

Franklin Roosevelt was the first president to recognize the power of Keynes's philosophy that government has a positive powerful role to play as buyer of last resort to provide employment and prosperity to all its citizens. Although Roosevelt was still hampered by fears of a national debt overwhelming the nation, when the Second World War broke out such fears were brushed aside. Spending sufficiently to assure the winning of the war, financed by huge government deficits, proved beyond a shadow of a doubt that the government could always play an active role in guaranteeing full employment prosperity for its business enterprises and its labor force. If there is sufficient market demand for their products, even if available workers lack sufficient skill for a particular job this is not an unsurmountable problem. All that is required is to provide on-the-job training. For example, during the Second World War, many young men left the civilian workforce to become members of the armed forces. Accordingly, there was a shortage of men in the civilian labor force to do many jobs that until then only men were considered capable of doing. When enterprise saw that market demand was strong enough to profitably employ many more in these "men's" jobs, entrepreneurs recruited women and provided them with on-the-job training to do these jobs. Thus, for example, women became skilled riveters who helped build warships, tanks, planes, and so on. In the earlier peacetime economy, these women were primarily educated with the skills to be a housewife.

Republican and Democratic successors to Roosevelt adopted variations of Keynes's policy initiatives to maintain economic prosperity, even if they did not necessarily recognize that these policy prescriptions were first suggested by Keynes. As we have already noted, President Truman's Administration produced the Marshall Plan where the United States as the major international trade surplus nation used its wealth to solve the post war trade imbalance problem. The Marshall Plan created job opportunities in export industries for American workers while also helping the European nations, whether they were allies or former enemies, to rebuild their national economies.

President Eisenhower succeeded Truman to the presidency. Eisenhower instituted one of the largest peacetime public works programs ever undertaken: the building of the interstate highway system. Not only did construction of the interstate highway system create profits and jobs in the construction and related industries, but it also provided the nation with a transportation system that increased the productivity of American factories by making it less expensive to take delivery of raw materials at the factory door and less expensive to deliver the finished product to the market place. The result of such active government policies was to make the United States and most of the free world a more prosperous and civilized place in which to live.

Meanwhile, during these years, the Federal Reserve recognized that its primary function was to maintain the liquidity and stability of financial markets, while at the same time the Glass–Steagall Act was strictly enforced so that the banking function of making nonresalable loans to customers was legally separated from the underwriting function of investment bankers to sell securities in well-organized and orderly financial markets.

With the advent of Stagflation in the 1970s and the victory of the classical free market philosophy over the perverted view of Keynesianism that appeared in textbooks such as written by Paul Samuelson after the Second World War, central banks and governments began to adopt a different, less civilized philosophical policy approach to the economy. In 1979, for example, after a second spike in crude oil prices engineered by OPEC, the Federal Reserve, under Chairman Paul Volker, raised interest rates to double digit levels to deliberately destroy profit opportunities for many businesses and to create the highest unemployment rate since the Great Depression. This stopped the wage incomes inflation process in its tracks.

As the US economy tumbled downward in 1979 and the rest of the free world's economies also collapsed, there was a severe drop in the demand for gasoline and other petroleum products. Simultaneously, new non-OPEC crude oil supplies were coming onto the markets from regions such as the North Sea and Alaska. The result was that the OPEC cartel could not continue to exert as much cartel power in the market and oil prices dropped and remained low for many years into the future. The threat of a commodity inflation inducing incomes inflation as workers demanded cost of living increases induced by rising energy prices and businesses raising prices to protect their profit margins from inflation seemed to be tamed.

The lesson taken away from this 1979–1981 Federal Reserve induced recession episode of a deliberate policy to create high unemployment to end a period of incomes inflation was simple, and it fitted the free market philosophy of conservative economic theory. An independent central bank board of governors, whose members were not subject to political elections every two years, could make independent tight monetary policies that the public would have to accept, even though the results of collapsing profit opportunities and a large increase in unemployment devastated many members of the population. It was recognized that central bank tight money policies would be aimed at constraining inflationary forces that are unleashed when the economy becomes so prosperous that workers and managers believe that, in a free market, they can raise wages and prices without losing customers.

Instead, this classical economic theory suggested that central bank policy should and would be designed so that if the inflation rate was larger than the central bankers believed desirable, then the central bank had the responsibility to institute a high interest rate, tight money policy deliberately aimed at producing fewer profit opportunities for business firms. This would induce employers to lay off many workers. The result was to make workers and their unions more docile and willing to accept stagnant or even falling money wage rates. Monetary policy was often seen as "the only game in town" to control inflation and unemployment levels.

Andrew Mellon's classical theory's philosophical message to President Hoover was back in the corridors of power. In the 1970s, to purge the rottenness out of the system (i.e., high incomes inflation) required liquidating businesses' and workers' income earning opportunities. With this loss of income opportunities, enterprise and workers will work harder and demand less when a job or profit opportunity, in the long run, does reappear. Surely this Mellon philosophy approach is not a civilized solution to the economic problems of a 21st-century capitalist system.

Keynes's solution was simple and certainly more civilized. As long as people want to work, the government must make sure that they have an opportunity to obtain a job fitting to their skills and, if necessary, obtain new skills via on-the-job training. If there is sufficient demand from private sector buyers to create market demand for all the goods and services that the nation's business firms can produce with a fully employed labor force, then the government's only responsibility is to make sure that employers are obeying the laws that a civilized society enacts to ensure safe working conditions, product safety requirements and so on.

If, and only if, there is a significant shortfall in market demand for products of the nation's industries, then the government should take an active role in pumping up market demand to create profit opportunities for businesses and job opportunities for the otherwise unemployed. When a significantly large recession appears on the economic horizon and private sector buyers remain reluctant to spend additional sums, then the government must step in to act as the purchaser of last resort.

Keynes argued that the government should attempt to spend in those areas that are investments in productivity enhancing activities that will provide useful goods and services for the population. If government spending appears to be "the only means of securing an approximation to full employment ... this need not exclude all manner of compromises and devices by which the public authority will co-operate with private initiative."[1]

Accordingly, government financing of the rebuilding of the economic infrastructure by building and repairing the nation's highways, bridges, airports, harbors and so on are clearly productive investments that can be accomplished by government letting contracts to private enterprise.[2] Other infrastructure projects that

would contribute to improving the health and therefore the productive life of the nation's citizens include the repair and improvement
of water supply systems and sanitary facilities of all kinds. Spending to develop light rail transportation systems to promote moving
commuter traffic to reliable public transportation will reduce the
use of automobiles that often clog our city streets and highways.
Such projects will also contribute to the nation's effort to prevent
global warming and reduce the pollution of the atmosphere that we
leave to our children and grandchildren.

Government spending on better education for all its citizens is
obviously desirable as an investment in making our system a more
civilized one with a skilled and intelligent population. This spending to provide a better useful education can take many forms. In the
1930s, for example, President Roosevelt created the Civilian Conservation Corps (CCC). This institution took unemployed young
men off the streets of the cities and moved them to areas like
Appalachia where they were housed and fed. In the Appalachian
forests, these young men were taught to do jobs requiring skills
such as building houses, roads and parks. The result was a labor
force that was educated to do many crafts that would be demanded
as the economy recovered from the Great Depression.

In our high-tech global economy of the 21st century, education is
an especially important investment project for developing the skills,
knowledge and pleasures of future generations. With local governments incurring significant shortfalls in their tax receipts, local
governments find it difficult, if not impossible, to even maintain the
present educational system, much less upgrade the educational
system. If the federal government would provide funding for local
and state educational systems, our public schools, public community colleges and public universities could become the platform
for launching our citizens into a more productive life.

Government spending can also encourage research and development by universities and private sector business firms for better
products and for new procedures to better protect the population
from diseases.

If, however, as Keynes warned, "we are so sensible ... taking
careful thought before we add to the 'financial' burdens of prosperity by building [productive investment for them to use, then] ... we
have no such easy escape from the sufferings of unemployment."[3]
Those who argue that the government should not borrow to create

jobs and make productive investments for future generations to use, because the borrowing will impoverish future generations with debts, do not realize how much we will impoverish future generations by not providing these productive outcomes if the government does nothing in order to pass on a smaller national debt to posterity.

Clearly, the list of possible investment projects that government can encourage with a significant spending recovery plan is enormous. Many of these projects would be desirable to invest in even if the economy was not in a significant recession. The opportunities for improving the productivity of our citizens are too obvious to not take advantage of them because of the argument that the resulting national debt will be too burdensome for our children.

Probably an important, but potentially politically controversial, project involves investing in the health care for all the citizens of the nation. Unlike most developed nations, until 2014 the United States did not have any national health program to protect the health of all is citizens. Instead, it relied on, and still relies on, a patchwork of various health insurance programs, which gained even more force with the passage of the Affordable Care Act, that is, Obamacare.

During the Second World War, many employers provided fringe benefits such as health insurance plans to recruit workers. These private health insurance plans for workers, financed by employers, have been the major form of national health insurance for decades. This way of providing health insurance adds significantly to the business firm's costs of producing and selling its products. It has been suggested that for the Big Three US automakers, the cost of health care for their employees and retirees (whose health care costs are also covered) per automobile produced is greater than the cost of steel used in producing each automobile. This clearly puts employers at a tremendous competitive cost disadvantage relative to producing cars in foreign nations, especially in an era where free international trade is being foisted on the public.

All retired workers who are over 65 years of age may be covered by the government's Medicare health plan. For households whose workers are not covered by employee health insurance plans, and for those unemployed for any length of time, the only way to obtain health care coverage is to purchase private health insurance. Statistics indicate that before Obamacare millions of Americans were without any health plan coverage and therefore did not go to doctors for preventive medicine. At least since Obamacare in 2014, all residents of the United States should have some form of medical insurance, although the costs of administrating these many different plans are significantly greater than the costs associated with a single payer system such as Medicare.

It should be obvious that to participate and flourish in our economic system access to health care is a priority. Good health increases productivity and longevity. As Stephen P. Dunn, a senior strategy adviser to the UK's Department of Health and Director of Provider Development of the National Health Service East of England, states: "Reduction in avoidable disease and increases in years of healthy life expectancy would accelerate economic growth … . The economic loss to society of shortened lives due to early death and chronic disability is hundreds of billions of dollars per year."[4]

An important idea that a civilized society should face is that health care is more than a basic right for every member of the community. If every person is going to effectively contribute to the productive activities of the nation, and if this contribution is to be done well, then the individual and the members of his/her family must be as healthy as the practice and technological advances of medicine permit.

A civilized society recognizes the basic right of all its members to find employment where they can use their talents to turn out the best possible product. Surely there is an argument to consider whether access to health care, paid by the community at large rather by employers and individuals, can improve the productivity of workers and thereby benefit the community. For healthier workers are always more productive workers. Keynes does not have a facile solution to the question of whether all members of society are entitled to health care independent of their income. But surely there is some evidence which indicates that access to universal health care independent of a family's income would be a productive investment for society to undertake.

In sum, there is a significantly large number of investment projects that government can finance by spending to encourage the private sector to produce results. The problem is not a shortage of financing; the problem is often a shortage of political resolve to take on such productive spending policies by government.

Finally, we have hopefully demonstrated to our readers that government regulators have an important role to play in assuring the members of our society that public financial markets are well organized and orderly. Furthermore, participants in financial markets should be required to provide contracts that deal fairly and honestly with other participants. This will protect households who are searching for financial assets in which to place their savings in order to meet any future spending plans (whether anticipated or not) during their active income earning period plus provide sufficient liquid purchasing power in their retirement years.

The task of putting our Keynes–Post Keynesian solution into practice will not be easy. It, however, offers more hope for a stable prosperous economic system than the efficient market philosophy of classical economic theory that has been promoted in recent decades. The latter has brought us again to the brink of economic disaster. We can only hope the public and our politicians learn from this book that there are better ways of achieving a good economic life for all citizens than merely trusting to a free market to solve our problems.

NOTES

1. J. M. Keynes, *The General Theory of Employment, Interest and Money* (Macmillan, London, 1936) p. 378.
2. Statistics indicate that in America there are a large number of bridges and highways that are urgently in need of repair.
3. Op. cit., p. 131.
4. S. P. Dunn, *The "Uncertain" Foundation of Post Keynesian Economics* (Routledge, London, 2008) p. 187.

Index

accounting periods 38–9
Affordable Care Act 142–3
aggregate demand 11, 29, 47, 49, 53, 61–2, 65, 71, 125
animal spirits 54
Arrow, K.J. 17, 25, 30, 31
assets
    derivative 3–4, 6
    perceived high degree of liquidity 84–5, 87–8
    toxic 4
    see also financial assets; illiquid assets; liquid assets
astronomy, ergodic theory 18–19
auction rate security markets 77, 84, 90
austerity 32, 51, 76
automatic mechanism of adjustment 46, 106, 110
axioms 8–9
    see also classical axioms

balance of trade 94, 96–8, 100, 116
bank credit 64–5
    see also overdrafts
bank deposits 4, 29–30, 31–2, 109–10
banking systems 64, 72, 82–3, 108, 109, 114
bankruptcy 33, 56, 59
Bear Stearns 82–3
bearishness 3–4, 35, 83
bears 35, 117
Berlin Wall 104
Bernanke, B. 94
Blanchard, O. 22

bonds 2, 3, 23, 79, 82, 89, 107
borrowing 53–6, 59, 64, 94–5, 111, 142
    see also overdrafts
Bretton Woods 99–105, 108, 113
Britain *see* United Kingdom
Bryce, R. 44–5, 48
Buckley, W. 43
buffer stocks 68–9
bull-bear sentiment 117
Bush, George H.W. 89
buy orders 78, 81

capital 19, 79, 98–9, 102, 104–5, 118–19, 124, 132–4
capital controls 99, 114–15, 117–18, 120
capital goods 2, 37–8, 48
capitalism 15, 60
capitalist economy 4–5, 9–10, 31, 33, 140
cartels 71, 129–30, 139
cash 2–3, 81–5, 88–90, 136
cash flow debt obligations 79
cash inflows 31–2, 34
central bankers 9, 14, 23, 35, 64, 117, 139
central banks
    change in policy approach to economy 138
    control of banking system 64, 72
    as created by federal government 56
    and IMCU 109, 114–15, 117, 119–22
    as inflation-curers 63, 139
    mainstream models, use of 22–3

market maker's access to 81, 83
monetary policy and employment
    64–5, 72–3
quantitative easing 89
certainty 16–17, 31, 33, 35, 79
    see also uncertainty
Chartalism 32–3
child labor 128, 133–4
China 71, 73, 93–8, 115–16, 134
Churchill, Winston 15
circuit breakers 35, 81
civil law of contracts 31, 34
Civilian Conservation Corps (CCC)
    141
civilized society/societies 61–2, 88,
    134, 136, 140, 143
classical axioms 9, 12–13
    overthrown by Keynes 15–16
        ergodic 16–21
        gross substitution 25
        Keynesianism based on 42
        neutral money 21–5
    Samuelson's foundations 48
classical economic theory
    affecting government decision
        making 41–2
    axiomatic foundations 15–25, 48
    central bank policy 139–40
    criticism by Keynes 29, 36, 47,
        106
    as fundamental economic theory 9
    incompatibility with international
        trade and finance 99
    and inflation 63, 72
    on international free trade 124
    vs. Keynes–Post Keynesian
        approach 4–5, 33, 137, 144
    law of comparative advantage
        124–7, 131–4
    Ricardian equivalence thesis 54
    on saving 30, 38
    and Say's Law 10–13
    and unemployment 15, 36, 41, 73,
        98
classification system 29

clearing price 77, 84, 86, 90
clearing union *see* International
    Monetary Clearing Union
    (IMCU)
Clinton, Bill 106–8
COLA (cost of living adjustment)
    clause 40
Colander, D.C. 43–4, 46
collateral 5, 82–3, 86
commodity inflation 66, 139
communication costs 128–31
comparative advantage, law of
    124–35
consumption
    of debtor nations 102–3
    Friedman's definition 38–9
    Keynes' definition 29, 39
    people gaining pleasure from
        10–11
contracts
    civil law of 31, 34
    fair and honest 144
    forward 65–7, 70
    government 140
    international 110, 119
    money 28–40, 65
    prices and inflation 65–7
    wage 69–70
    see also debt contracts
contractual obligations 24, 31–4, 56,
    119
contractual settlement 34, 95, 110
controls, capital 99, 114–15,
    117–18, 120
cost of living adjustment (COLA)
    clause 40
credit *see* bank credit; excessive
    credit
credit cards 53, 60
credit default swaps 77, 79, 80,
    90
creditor nations 95, 96, 100, 101,
    104–6, 119–20
currency 97, 107, 118–22

Davidson, P. 2, 4, 49, 90, 135
Dawes Plan 101
Debreu, G. 17
debt
    international 96–7, 100–104,
        106–7, 111–13, 120, 123
    long-term instruments 79, 86
    national 56–62, 137, 141–2
    of US government 55–62, 95–6
debt contracts 32, 56, 79, 112, 120
decision makers 16–17, 25, 30–34,
        39, 41–2, 54–5
deficits
    current account 120
    current policies for 51
    government 53–6, 58–9, 61, 137
    international payments 104, 106,
        107
    quantitative easing for 23
    trade 94, 98, 111–13
deflation 63–4, 66, 67, 69, 72
delivery 65–8, 128, 138
demand
    aggregate *see* aggregate demand
    domestic 125–6
    economic growth driven by 125
    effective 47–50, 121, 131
    expansion of trade driven by 131
    and full employment 46, 55
    inability of supply to create its
        own 12, 28–9
    of labor 65, 71–6, 139–40
    for money 36–7
    for producibles 37–8, 52, 56,
        60–61, 66–8, 92–3, 97–8,
        110, 113, 132, 140
    supply creating its own 10, 11
    and unemployment 28, 36, 53
democracy 15
deregulation 7, 137
derivative securities 3–4, 6–7, 32,
        77, 82–4, 87, 89–90, 108, 115,
        136
Desert Storm war 68–9

direct foreign investment 111–12,
        119
Dunlop, J.G. 46
Dunn, S.P. 143
durable goods 25, 26–7, 32, 34, 35,
        38, 40, 66

education 56, 134, 141
efficient market theory (EMT) 9, 19,
        77–80, 90, 97
Einstein, A. 24
Eisenhower, Dwight D. 59, 138
elasticity of production 36–7, 39
elasticity of substitution 36, 37,
        39
employment
    effect of changes in quantity of
        money 22–3
    general theory of 12
    government role 137
    liquidity theory of 30
    and Marshall Plan 104
    and non-employment inducing
        demand 37–8
    in relation to health care 143
    and trading partner nations 93,
        95–6, 109, 128–9, 134
    understanding role of liquidity
        24
    see also full employment;
        unemployment
ergodic axiom 16–21, 33, 48, 79–80,
        90
Euclidean geometers analogy 12,
        24
Europe 100–103, 105, 138
excessive credit 110–13, 119–20,
        123
exchange rates 98–9, 120, 122

Federal Reserve 23, 82–3, 89–90,
        97–8, 138–9
financial assets 2–4, 33, 55, 78–9,
        83–4, 89–90

financial crisis (2007–2008) 1, 4, 6,
        14, 16, 19–20, 53, 77, 79–80,
        113, 136
financial markets
    distribution of buyers and sellers
        84
    efficiency of 16, 19–20, 79–80
    EMT of 78–80
    exotic 77
    Greenspan's theory of 8
    and market makers 35
    and need for liquidity 31, 138
    new financial architecture for 107
    in pre-computer age 78
    primary function of 33, 80–81
    prior to financial crisis 1, 3
    and regulation policy 85–90
    use of Post Keynesian analytical
        system 4
    well-organized 2, 144
    see also free markets
fire analogy 107, 113
Fischer, S. 107
flight capital 114
foreign aid 103–4, 106, 111–12, 120
foreign reserves 35, 94, 100–101,
        110–11, 120
forward contracts 65–7, 70
France 75, 108
free markets 6–7, 14, 25, 70–72,
        97–8, 106–7, 133, 136–9, 144
free trade 71, 99, 129–35
Friedman, M. 22–3, 26–7, 38–9
full employment
    and aggregate demand 29, 71
    cause of economy being at less
        than 28
    in classical economic theory 12,
        15, 21, 98
    equilibrium 25
    government interference 41
    government role 134, 136, 137,
        140
    IMCU encouraging 110–11
    and incomes policy 71, 72, 76

    and international trade 99, 132–3
    and Keynes' general theory 24–5,
        46–7, 49, 50, 64–5
    in post-war US 103–4
    and Say's Law 11, 39, 132
    see also employment;
        unemployment
fully liquid assets 35
"fundamentals" 19, 51, 77, 78,
        79–80, 90

G7 nations 107
Galbraith, J.K. 24, 70
"general equilibrium" 25, 30, 37, 43,
        47, 49
general theory 1–2, 12, 21, 24–5, 29,
        42–51, 52, 63–4, 92
*The General Theory of Employment,
        Interest and Money* (Keynes) 3,
        14, 20, 24, 25, 29, 36, 39, 42,
        44–7, 49, 63, 140
Germany 75, 101, 108
Glass–Steagall Act 89, 138
global financial crisis *see* financial
        crisis (2007–2008)
Goldman Sachs 82, 84–5
government
    borrowing to create 141–2
    decision making 41–2
    interference 10, 18–19, 41, 124,
        136
    investment projects 140–43
    policy
        assuring a civilized economic
            system 136–44
        capital controls 114–15
        creating full employment
            53–62, 71
        under ergodic axiom 18–19, 21
        foreign aid 106
        Keynes' rationale for role of 39
        on natural resource availability
            129
        promoting balanced
            government budgets 51

to reduce unemployment 28
reducing benefits 73
reducing taxes 75
regulation 6, 88, 124
see also United States:
government
Great Depression (1929) 2, 6, 11, 41,
58, 59, 70, 75, 139, 141
Greenspan, A. 6–9, 13–14, 16,
19–20
gross domestic product (GDP) 19,
22, 58–9, 61, 103, 129
gross substitution axiom 25, 48

Hahn, F.H. 25, 30, 31
Harrod, R.F. 29
Hayek, F. 45
health care 142–3
Hicks, J.R. 20
Hilsenrath, J. 23
Home Owners' Loan Corporation
(HOLC) 89
Hoover, H. 41–2, 140
households 4, 5, 33, 37–8, 53–60, 70,
92, 97–8, 103, 144

ignoratio elenchi 47
illiquid assets 32, 36, 83, 85, 87
IMCU *see* International Monetary
Clearing Union
IMF (International Monetary Fund)
4, 102, 107, 113
income
after-tax 54–5
enhancing 124–6, 132
inequalities 15, 51, 59, 74
principle 28
real 22, 97
and savings 32, 37–9, 40, 55–6
"time preference" 30
income earning 2, 5, 10–11, 30, 37,
52, 102, 109–10, 136, 140, 144
incomes inflation 66–7, 69–74, 139
incomes policy 67, 70–76
incomes policy of fear 73, 75

India 71, 73, 93–4, 130, 134
industrial reserve army 71, 73, 130
inflation 22–3, 40
contracts and prices 65–7
domestic 121
Federal Reserve policy 97–8
incomes 66–7, 69–74, 139
incomes policy 70–76
policy 63–5
process of 67–9
wage-price 120–121
International Monetary Clearing
Union
aims 108–9
cross border fund movements
114–15
and excessive credits 110–13,
119–20, 123
IMC Units 117–21
objectives 110
reinstating the global economy
113–14
requirements 109, 117–22
as variant of Keynes Plan 109–10
international payments 87–8, 91,
98–100
need for clearing institution 109
reformation 106–14, 117–22
United States 103, 104–5, 113
international trade
Bretton Woods solution 99–105
case for capital controls 114–15
demand driven expansion 131
hypothetical example 94
and law of comparative advantage
129
reforming international payments
system 106–14

J. P. Morgan Chase 82–3
Jackson, Andrew 57
Japan 93, 104–5
Johnson, Lyndon B. 59
Joseph (biblical) analogy 69

Kennedy, John Fitzgerald 59
Keynes, J.M. 2
    on aggregate demand 29
    on "animal spirits" 54
    axioms overthrown by 12–13,
        15–25
    on balance of trade 96–7
    on bank credit 64
    branches of Keynesianism 41–51
    on capitalism 15, 60
    civilized solution to economic
        problems 140, 141
    and classification 29
    on government fiscal policy 60
    on ideas of economists and
        philosophers 14
    on "knowing" the future 20, 33
    and law of comparative advantage
        129
    on liquid assets 36–7
    liquidity preference theory (LPT)
        36, 77, 80–85
    liquidity theory 9–10, 20, 30, 33
    on market demand 131
    on mass production processes
        across nations 127, 133
    and money contracts 30–33
    point on unemployment
        equilibrium 37
    principle on excessive credits 111,
        113
    Roosevelt's endorsement 137–8
    on savings 29–30, 37, 39
    on Say's Law 11–12, 29, 132
    on sufferings of unemployment
        141
    on tax cuts 54–5
    theory of inflation 63, 66, 74
    see also general theory
Keynes Plan 91, 99–102, 106, 108,
        109, 113–14
Keynes–Post Keynesian theory
    alternative to classical economic
        theory 137

    and central bank monetary policy
        64
    liquidity 9–10, 33
    money and money contracts
        28–39
    moral of 55
    savings and earnings 94
    solution into practice 144
    "knowing" the future 16–17, 19–20,
        31, 33, 34

labor
    cheap supply of 76, 128–9, 133–5
    civilized conditions for 128
    and comparative advantage 126–7
    costs of product 14, 63, 69, 123,
        130–31, 133
    effect of increased liquidity 36–7
    hiring contract 67
    liberalizing markets 73
    mobility 132
    monopoly elements not cause of
        unemployment 42
    non-competitive 41
    outsourcing 130
    protection in cheap foreign labor
        nations 75–6
    slack in market 65, 75
    and wage income demands 73–4
    wages contracts 70
    see also child labor; wages;
        workers
laissez-faire 19, 21, 71, 101, 106
Landreth, H. 43–4, 46
law of comparative advantage
        124–35
Lehman Brothers 84–5
liquid assets
    Chinese savers 95
    credit surplus nations 104, 110–11
    definition 35
    ease of becoming illiquid 84–5
    enhancing liquidity position 32,
        33

essential properties of 36–9, 42, 43
foreign 114
holding outstanding 83
IMC Units as 117
and savings 25, 29–30, 34–6
and tax cuts 55
types of 2
value of traded 79–81
liquidity
and central bank policy 64–5, 83
concept 31
excessive holdings 112, 120
of exotic assets 86–7
Federal Reserve's function 138
Keynes theory of 9–10, 20, 30, 33
and market makers 80–84
orderliness for 78
and quantitative easing 89–90
reserve asset for international 117
and savings 34–6
security cushion 32
understanding essential role of 24
liquidity crisis 3–4, 120
liquidity preference theory (LPT) 36, 77, 80–85
Long Term Capital Management (LTCM) hedge fund 107
Lucas, R. 17

mainstream theories 4, 9, 21–2, 30, 33, 41, 42–3, 50–51
market demand *see* demand
market failure 77–90
market makers 34–6, 78, 81–8, 98, 115
Marshall, A. 44, 46, 49, 63, 66, 76
Marshall Plan 103–5, 111, 138
Marx, K. 71
mass production processes 126–33
Mayer, M. 118
McCarthyism 43, 50
Mellon, A. 41–2, 140
Merrill Lynch 84–5

Mexico 68, 106–7
minimum wage legislation 15, 73, 129
monetary policy 53, 63–5, 72–3, 89, 97, 108, 118, 139
money
axiom of neutral 21–5, 48, 63–4
and money contracts 28–40, 65
quantity theory of 22
Moore, G.E. 29
mortgage backed derivatives 3, 6, 19, 23, 32, 77, 82, 84, 115, 136
Mr. Micawber 57

national debt 56–62, 137, 141–2
neoclassical synthesis Keynesianism 9, 21, 42–4, 48
neutral money axiom 21–5, 48, 63–4
New Keynesian theory 9, 21, 42–3
New York Stock Exchange 2, 6, 82
New York Times 84–5
Nixon, Richard 105–6
non-Euclidean economics 12, 24

Obama, Barack 19, 93, 107, 113
Obamacare 142–3
OECD nations 51, 72, 73, 134
oil market 68–9, 129–30, 138–9
OPEC (Organization of the Petroleum Exporting Countries) 129–30, 138–9
orderliness 33–6, 77–81, 85–7, 138, 144
outsourcing 73–5, 129–35
overdrafts 119

Panglossian conclusion 24
Post Keynesian analysis 4–5, 131
see also Keynes-Post Keynesian theory
Post Keynesians 1–2, 21, 30, 33, 54–5
price talk 84–5, 90
probability theory 17

propensity to save 39, 56

quantitative easing 23, 89–90
Queen Elizabeth II 1

Rappaport, L. 23
rating agencies 3, 86–7
rational expectations theory 17–18,
    33, 90
reconstructed Keynesians 50–51
regulation policy 85–90
research and development spending
    53–4, 131, 141
Resolution Trust Company (RTC)
    83, 89, 90
"resting places" 37, 39
Ricardian equivalence thesis 54
Ricardo, D. 125–7, 132
Robinson, J. 50
Roosevelt, Franklin D. 45, 58–60,
    89, 137–8, 141
Rubin, R. 106–7
Russia 107

Samuelson, P.A. 9, 21, 42–51, 138
Sargent, Thomas 18
savings
    definitions of 26–7, 38–9
    and income 32, 37–9, 40, 55–6
    Keynes on 29–30, 37, 39
    Keynes–Post Keynesian theory on
        94
    and liquid assets 25, 29–30
    and liquidity 34–6
Say, J.B. 10
Say's Law 10–13, 25, 29, 37–9, 132
SEC *see* Securities and Exchange
    Commission
Second World War
    government restrictions following
        130–31
    impact on Europe 100–102
    industrial society following 70–72
    situation in United States 58–9,
        61, 137, 142

Securities and Exchange
    Commission (SEC) 85–9, 115
securitization 3, 86, 88–9
securitized derivatives *see* derivative
    securities
sell orders 78, 81
serious monetary theory 30–31, 39
shocks 14, 21, 47–8, 68, 104–5
Smith, A. 124–5, 131
smoking 88
Soros, G. 33
spot prices 65–8, 76
Stagflation 138
stochastic process 17–20
stochastic system 80
stochastic theory 17
subprime mortgages 3, 5, 6, 77, 108,
    136
Summers, L. 19, 79–80
"supply creates its own demand" 10
sweatshops 128–9
sword analogy 2, 4

Tarshis, L. 43–4, 48
tax-based incomes policy (TIP)
    74–6
tax cuts 54–5, 93
tax revenues 54, 57–8, 61
terrorist attacks 61, 81–2
terrorist operations, financing 110,
    115
Thatcher, Margaret 72
theory
    alternative 9–10, 137
    as providing explanation 7–9
    and Say's Law 10–13
    see also individual theories
time preference 30
TIP (tax-based incomes policy) 74–6
trade *see* international trade
transportation costs 128–9, 131
Truman, Harry S. 103, 138

Uchitelle, L. 129, 134
uncertainty 20, 30–31, 34, 80–81

see also certainty
unemployment
    appropriate government policy 28
    cause of persistent 53
    and central bank policy 64
    and China's exports 95, 98
    and classical theory axioms 14–25
    classical theory explanation of
        41–2, 98
    and dissaving 55
    excessive credits creating 111,
        112
    Federal Reserve's induced
        recession 139
    and free trade 128, 134–5
    Keynes' explanation of 36–7, 39,
        42–3
    Keynes on sufferings of 141
    natural rate of 73
    rapid rise on entering Great
        Depression 58
    theories concerning 11–12
    and wages 65
unemployment equilibrium theory
    37, 39, 46–7
United Kingdom 63, 72, 108, 143
United States (US)
    exports 92–3
    government
        closing gold window 105
        confidence in, after terrorist
            attacks 81–2
        debt 55–62, 95–6
        military spending 103–4
        project financing 140–43
        stimulus bill 93
    imports 92–3
    international payments 103,
        104–5, 113
    as major surplus nation 138
    oil strategy 68–9, 129–30, 138–9
    and Second World War 58–9, 61,
        137, 142
unreconstructed Keynesians 50

Vietnam 59, 104
Volker, P. 138–9

wages
    accepting lower 13, 73–4
    and classical economic theory 13,
        15
    competitive 134–5
    demand for higher 65, 71–2
    efficiency 120–22
    flexible 10, 12, 14, 21, 37, 39, 42
    increases in 67, 69–70, 116
    in mass production industries
        127–8, 130–31
    and outsourcing 130
    in personal service industries
        128–9
    "real" 40
    rigidity of 15, 36, 44–7
    stickiness 15, 46
    see also labor; workers
Wall Street Journal 23, 82
Walras, L. 9, 16–17, 44, 45, 50
Walrasian general equilibrium 25,
    43, 47–9
Walrasian system 16–17, 21, 44–6
Walrasian theory 9, 30, 42–51
wealth of nations 124–5, 131
Weintraub, S. 49–51, 74–5
White, H.D. 101–2, 103
White Plan 102–3
wine-cloth example 126–7
workers
    and central bank policy 139
    and classical economic theory
        140
    COLA clause 40
    displaced 134–5
    governments spending less, effect
        on 59–60
    health insurance for 142–3
    hiring of 28, 36–7, 53, 60–62, 64,
        92
    and incomes policy 71–6
    on-the-job training 137

Keynes' explanation of 12–13, 52, 137
labor contracts 67
and Marshall Plan 110–11, 138
in mass production industries 128–9, 132
refusing to accept lower wages 12–13, 15

and Say's Law 11, 29
and tax cuts 55
US and Chinese 95–6, 98, 116
see also labor; wages
World Bank 102, 113
World War II *see* Second World War